Playful

Corey Yoder

Learn Simple, Fusible Appliqué

Petals

18 Quilted Projects Made From Precuts

stashBOOKS.

an imprint of C&T Publishing

Text copyright © 2014 by Corey Yoder

Photography and Artwork copyright © 2014 by C&T Publishing, Inc.

Publisher: Amy Marson

Creative Director: Gailen Runge

Art Director / Book Designer: Kristy Zacharias

Editor: Lynn Koolish

Technical Editors: Helen Frost and Gailen Runge

Production Coordinators: Jenny Davis and Karen Ide

Production Editor: Alice Mace Nakanishi

Illustrator: Jessica Jenkins

Photo Assistant: Mary Peyton Peppo

Photo Stylist: Lauren Toker

Instructional photography by Diane Pedersen, unless otherwise noted; **Style photography** by Nissa Brehmer, unless otherwise noted

Published by Stash Books, an imprint of C&T Publishing, Inc., P.O. Box 1456, Lafayette, CA 94549

Library of Congress Cataloging-in-Publication Data

Yoder, Corey, 1978-

 Playful petals : learn simple, fusible appliqué : 18 quilted projects made from precuts / Corey Yoder.

     pages cm

 ISBN 978-1-60705-797-0 (soft cover)

1. Appliqué--Patterns. 2. Fusible materials in sewing. I. Title.

 TT779.Y63 2014

 746.44'5--dc23

                          2013027056

Printed in China

10 9 8 7 6 5 4 3 2 1

Acknowledgments

Thank you to my husband, Ryan, and daughters, Chloe and Elonie, for putting up with seemingly endless hours of sewing.

Huge thanks go out to my personal cheerleader, my mom. She has never failed to encourage me in any endeavor I've wished to undertake and is always willing to help when I get in over my head.

Thank you to C&T Publishing for helping me realize my goal of becoming an author and for your willingness to work with a complete newbie.

I'd also like to thank Moda Fabrics, Riley Blake Fabrics, FreeSpirit Fabrics, and RJR Fabrics for generously providing me with fabric to use in this book.

Contents

Introduction

My love of appliqué began about fifteen years ago, prompted by my love of fabric. I began purchasing fabric before I had ever even touched a sewing machine or knew how to sew. There is just nothing like that fresh-from-the-bolt fabric smell, the vibrant prints, and the bright colors ... yes, I was hooked. The obvious outlet for my fabric-loving self was in the world of quiltmaking. My mom was both a quilt piecer and quilter, as were my grandma, my great-grandma, and others further back than that I am sure. Combine that fact with growing up in an Amish community—where quiltmaking is certainly an art, handmade items are prized, and small family fabric shops abound—and of course I fell in love with the world of quilts.

The first "quilt" I made involved 10 yards of $1.00 Grinch flannel. It was the first time I had used a sewing machine, and the quilt didn't involve any piecing. I gave it to my husband for Christmas on one of the first Christmases we shared. We still use it every day. The second quilt I made was a simple rag quilt using scrappy flannel homespun fabrics sewn together at my mom's house, with a ton of help from her, using her sewing machine (at this point, I didn't have one of my own). Then came quilt number three, a coin quilt featuring traditional appliqué and raw-edge appliqué. I agonized over every step, from choosing the right fabrics for the quilt pattern to piecing it perfectly and completing the appliqué. Once again, I pieced the quilt top at my mom's house, but this time all on my own. Shortly thereafter, I purchased my trusty Bernina, and she's been with me ever since.

That first appliquéd quilt quickly led to one more, followed by several more. This led to the opening of my appliquéd children's clothing business, and then on to quilt design. Through it all, appliqué has always played a primary role in my designs. I hope that as you look through the projects in this book and try your hand at some of the designs, you will come to love appliqué as much as I do!

In designing the projects in this book, I have kept the piecing simple to allow the appliqué to shine. All the projects have been designed using just one appliqué shape, a simple petal. There are no reverse templates, additional template seam allowances, or time-consuming methods to worry about. The projects are perfect for beginning quiltmakers as well as experienced quiltmakers who wish to broaden their quilting repertoire.

Appliqué Basics

Appliqué is simply the process of creating a design by layering one fabric (the design) over another (the background). There are many different ways to do this. For the projects in this book, you will be using paper-backed fusible web—permanent, heat-activated fabric glue sold by the yard or by the sheet.

tip *If you already make quilts, paper-backed fusible web is most likely the only additional item you will need to purchase to begin to appliqué.*

FUSIBLE WEB

There are many different brands of fusible web, including those with paper backing and those without. Heat*n*Bond, Wonder-Under, SoftFuse, and Trans-Web are examples of paper-backed fusible web. The paper backing provides a protective barrier between your iron and the fusible, eliminating the need for an appliqué pressing sheet. It also provides the perfect surface for tracing the appliqué template pieces. My personal favorite, and the fusible web I turn to most often, is Heat*n*Bond Lite, followed closely by Heat*n*Bond FeatherLite. No matter which brand of fusible web you use, for the most part opt for the lightest weight available from that brand. This eliminates extra bulk, which is important because you will be stacking up multiple layers of fabric. A lighter-weight fusible also allows all the raw edges to be finished with a sewing machine.

Because paper-backed fusible web is so easy to use, it will always be my number one choice, and the project instructions within this book are written for paper-backed fusible web. Should you be more comfortable using a paperless fusible, adapt the instructions accordingly and remember to use an appliqué pressing sheet or Silicone Release Paper (by C&T Publishing).

NOTE

Many fusible web products, when sold by the yard, are 17″ wide. Yardages for the projects in the book are based on that width. If the brand you purchase happens to be a bit wider, save the excess; small extra pieces are perfect for small projects such as pillows.

FABRIC

Choose good-quality fabric for your projects, both for the background and for the appliqué. Lightweight fabrics, such as muslin, voile, and knits, are more difficult to work with and require extra prep work to make them substantial enough to use as an appliqué background. There's a whole chapter on fabric (page 22) that gives you much more information.

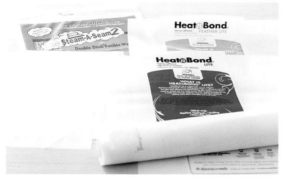

Fusible web

tip — *When purchasing fusible web, always purchase by the yard or by the roll if possible. Try to avoid prepackaged folded fusible web. The adhesive along the edges of fusible web that is folded in packages can deteriorate over time.*

PENCIL, PAPER, SCISSORS

The first step in fusible appliqué is to transfer the pattern onto the fusible web. Because you are working with symmetrical petals that do not need additional seam allowances added, this step is quite simple. Find the desired petal, place the fusible web *paper side up* on top of the petal pattern, and trace. The quilt projects in this book all use a number of petals, so follow the petal placement guide when tracing the petals and adjust as needed based on the size of the petals.

Petal placement guide: Place petals approximately ¼" apart.

After you have traced the desired number of petals, cut them out. Cut each petal out approximately ⅛" from the traced lines. To reduce stiffness in the finished quilt, remove the center portion of each petal. Cut through the edge of each petal to about ¼" inside the traced line and trim away the center, leaving a ring of fusible web in the shape of the petal.

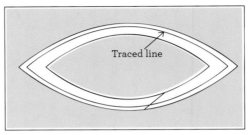

Traced line

Trim away center of fusible to reduce stiffness.

tip Set aside a pair of scissors specifically for cutting the paper-backed appliqué pieces. A fabric scissors will become dulled much more quickly when cutting paper.

FUSING

Most fusible web products advise you to prewash the fabrics prior to fusing. I do not prewash any of my fabrics when I make quilts, and I always opt to skip this step. I have never had a problem with the fusible not adhering to the fabric I am using. If you do have trouble with the fusible adhering properly to the fabric, I recommend prewashing the fabrics, as the chemicals in unwashed fabric can repel the adhesive.

The fusible web is now ready to fuse onto the fabric. Set your iron for the heat and steam requirements stated in the manufacturer's instructions for the brand of fusible web you are using. Place the petals *paper side up* on the *wrong side of the fabric* and iron them.

Make sure to iron on the paper side—the side with the traced lines visible. Most types of fusible web will take only a couple of seconds to fuse, but again, check the brand-specific requirements.

> *tip* *If you do a lot of appliqué, it is inevitable that at some point your iron will get some of the fusible web glue stuck to it. What to do? Iron a dryer sheet on low, with no steam. The residue should come right off. If you don't have dryer sheets, Dritz Iron Cleaner is a great product to have on hand to clean up any appliqué residue on your iron.*

After ironing the fusible web onto the fabric, cut the petals out on the traced line and remove the paper backing. They are now ready to fuse to the background. Place the background fabric right side up on your ironing board and arrange the petals, glue side down. Iron the petals to fuse them, again noting the fusible web brand-specific ironing instructions.

> *tip* *If the appliqué is not sticking, make sure your iron is the correct temperature—an iron that is too cool will not activate the adhesive. However, an iron that is too hot will deactivate the glue. If the temperature is correct and the appliqué is still not sticking, try prewashing your fabrics.*

STITCHING THE APPLIQUÉS

Lightweight fusible web, though permanent, needs a bit of help to make sure that appliqués are permanently attached. The fusible web is designed to hold the appliqué pieces in place until they can be stitched down. In the projects presented in this book, all the edges of the appliqué pieces will be finished with machine stitching after they have been ironed into place.

Choosing Thread

When it comes to thread for appliqué, the choices seem to be endless. More often than not, when I choose thread, I choose based on color preference rather than brand preference. I often choose Gütermann 100% polyester thread simply because of its availability and wide range of colors. I have also had great luck using 100% cotton Aurifil. The debate about using polyester or cotton thread seems to be fairly evenly split. My best suggestion is to use whatever thread works well for you and your machine. Try several different types and choose your favorite.

If you want the appliqué stitches to pop, choose a contrasting thread color in a heavier weight, such as 28- or 30-weight. To minimize the appliqué stitches, choose a coordinating thread color in a lighter weight, such as 50-weight.

> *tip* *For a uniform appliqué stitch, match the thread color in the bobbin to the top thread color. Otherwise you may notice contrasting colors in the stitching.*

Appliqué Stitches

Any number of stitches can be used to finish the petal edges.
I most often use a blanket stitch. This is a standard stitch on
many sewing machines and can be set to a number of widths
and lengths. In general, the stitch length is set slightly longer
than the stitch bite (width). A shorter bite works well for projects
that will not receive a lot of wear, while a deeper bite is better
for projects that will receive more use and wash wear.

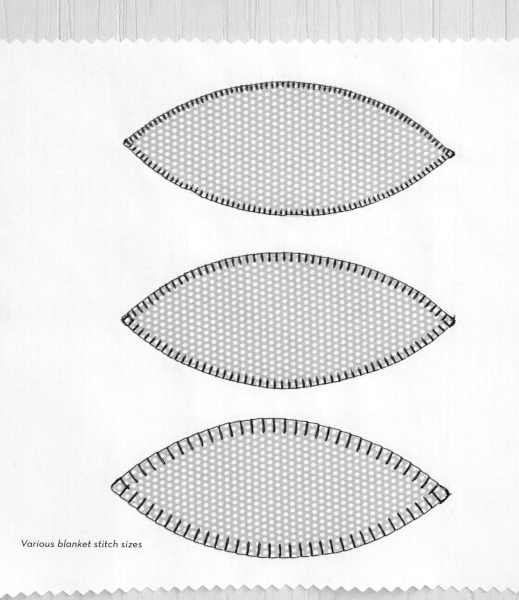

Various blanket stitch sizes

If the blanket stitch isn't your thing or if your machine isn't equipped with a blanket stitch, a straight stitch or zigzag stitch can be used instead. Be aware that appliqués stitched with a straight stitch will fray more when washed than will appliqués finished with a blanket or zigzag stitch.

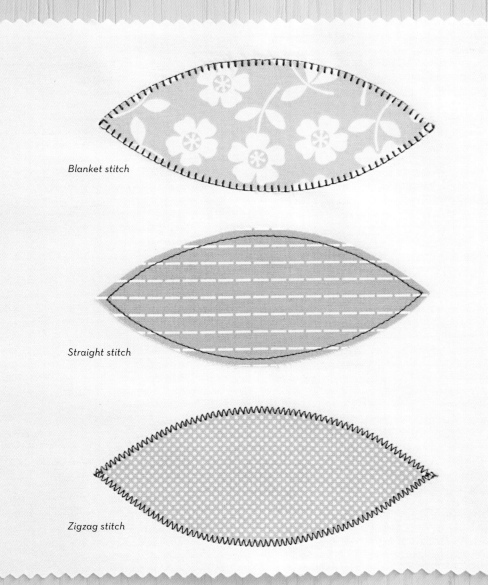

Blanket stitch

Straight stitch

Zigzag stitch

Stitching

The petals have been fused to the background, your sewing machine is in good working order, you've got the right color of thread, and you have a full bobbin of coordinating thread. You are ready to stitch ... almost.

Your choice of needles is important. Choose a needle based on the weight of the thread you are using. An 80/12 sharp (sometimes known as a Microtex sharp) is generally a great choice unless you are using a heavyweight thread.

1. Attach an open-toe presser foot to your sewing machine and set the needle to end in the down position if possible. Begin at the point of the petal by stitching several stitches in place or use a lockstitch, if your machine is so equipped, to anchor the thread. Set your machine to the stitch of your choice in the desired width and length and begin to stitch around the edge of the appliqué. The stitch should run along the outside edge of the petal, with the bite going toward the center.

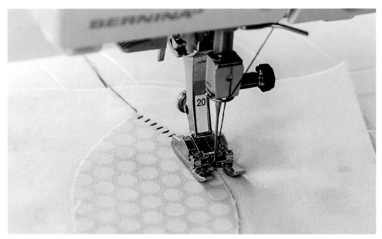

Stitch along edge of appliqué.

tip *If you notice that the stitching and/or fabric are bunching as you are stitching, stop and adjust the thread tension before you go any further.*

2. Stitch to the opposite petal point and end with the needle down at the point at the end of a stitch length. Raise the presser foot (keep the needle down), pivot the fabric, and complete stitching down the other side of the appliqué, ending where you started. Complete the petal appliqué by anchoring the stitching with several stitches in place or a lockstitch.

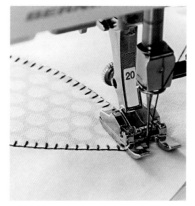

Stitch second side and end with lockstitch.

> *tip* Take your time as you near the point of the petal to make sure you don't zip right on by it. You can also manually sew the last stitch or two so they line up perfectly until you get the feel for your machine.
>
> As you complete the blanket stitch on the first side of the petal, be sure to end with the needle down at the very point. When you pivot and begin stitching down the other side, you will have perfect stitches at the point of the petal.

It may take a couple of tries until you are satisfied with the look of your appliqué stitches. Keep in mind that you are looking at your stitching very closely as you appliqué. Once the appliqué is completed within the quilt, an errant appliqué stitch will not even be noticed.

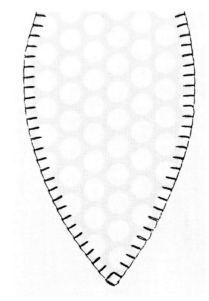

Perfect stitches at point

Pick Up the Pace

Appliquéing one petal at a time can feel time consuming. When possible, continue from one petal to the next without stopping in between petals. This eliminates the need to anchor the end of each petal as well as the beginning of the next petal. It also provides a seamless transition from one petal to the next.

Here are some guidelines: If the tips of four petals meet in the center, forming a four-petaled flower, begin stitching in the center. Stitch down the right edge of one petal to the petal tip. Pivot and begin stitching the other side of the petal, through the center, and around the right edge of the next petal to the outer petal tip. Pivot and continue in this manner until the appliqué is complete, ending in the center. Each continuous pass will form a half-circle.

If the petals form a circle, begin stitching at an outer point. Stitch around the perimeter of the petals, making a complete circle. Next complete the inner petal edges, pivoting slightly at each tip. Work your way back to the original starting point.

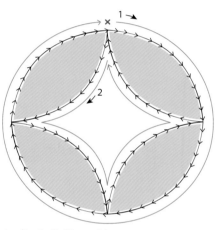

Appliqué stitching guide

Be sure to anchor the first petal in a series and the last petal in a series. You will notice diagrams throughout the book showing the most efficient way to complete the appliqué. The diagrams will work for a blanket stitch or zigzag stitch; however, straight-stitch appliqué must be done one petal at a time. When stitching one petal at a time, always begin and end the appliqué stitching at the tip closest to the block center.

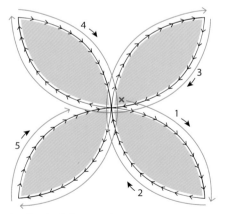

Appliqué stitching guide

Piecing

TOOLS OF THE TRADE

In addition to the supplies needed to appliqué, there are a few extra supplies you will need in order to complete the projects in this book.

Tools for piecing

Rotary Cutters, Mats, and Rulers

This trio of sewing items is probably the greatest time-saver, second only to your trusty sewing machine. I have a large 33″ × 58″ tabletop cutting mat, which I use most often, in conjunction with a 4″ × 36″ ruler and a 6½″ × 18½″ ruler. I also have a smaller 16½″ × 22½″ cutting mat I use for smaller projects. Choose either a 45mm or a 60mm rotary cutter.

Pins

I prefer longer, very thin pins to use when piecing. If they are cute (such as flower-head pins), that's an added bonus!

Fabric Scissors

A dedicated fabric scissors is essential.

Thread

I often use Gütermann thread to piece with, as I have it on hand all the time.

Curved Safety Pins and/or Temporary Fabric Spray Adhesive

I use curved safety pins to baste large projects for quilting and spray adhesive for small projects.

Water-Soluble Marker

I always have a Dritz Mark-B-Gone blue water-soluble marker on hand. I use it for marking quilting lines as well as appliqué placement lines.

Seam Ripper

I have several different seam rippers of various designs in my sewing arsenal. The one I use most often is the one I find first.

tip Whip up a cute pincushion for your cute pins.

A FEW TRICKS OF THE TRADE

The piecing for all the projects in this book is simple enough for beginners. Keep in mind good quiltmaking basics to ensure a great end project.

¼" Seam Allowance

An accurate ¼" seam allowance is essential to a beautiful finished project.

You have probably heard references to a "scant" ¼" seam allowance. The reason quilters use a seam allowance just a hair smaller than ¼" is because the thread and the fold of the seam take up a bit of space in each pieced block.

To check the accuracy of your ¼" seam, do the following:

1. Cut 3 strips of fabric 1½" wide by approximately 4" long.

2. Sew the 3 strips together side by side using a ¼" seam allowance (or what you think to be a ¼" seam allowance).

3. Press the seams away from the center.

4. Measure the block. It should measure 3½" wide.

If the measurement is wider than 3½", your seam allowance is too narrow. If the block is smaller than 3½", your seam allowance is too wide. To correct the seam allowance, move the needle position to the left or right as needed, if your machine is so equipped. Another option is to place a piece of tape ¼" to the right of the needle as a sewing guide, but do not cover the feed dogs.

After making the necessary adjustments, sew together another set of test strips to double-check your accuracy. If your machine is equipped with a ¼" foot, I would still encourage you to test your seam allowance for accuracy.

Pinning

I am not always an avid pinner. However, many of the projects in this book require pinning to ensure that all the points and petals line up as they should. As you pin the blocks together, make sure that all seams, as well as all petals, line up as shown.

Pressing

You've pinned, you've sewn, and now it's time to press. Make sure that you are in fact *pressing*. Pressing is lifting and placing the iron where it needs to be, as opposed to sliding it from place to place while on the fabric (ironing). Pressing will not distort the block shape. Adjacent seams are typically pressed in opposite directions to create locking or nesting seams.

tip *You will notice that several of the projects in this book require the seams to be pressed open. To press the seams open, first press them gently to one side using your iron; then press them open.*

tip *Need more piecing help?* Simplify *by Camille Roskelley and* The Practical Guide to Patchwork *by Elizabeth Hartman (both from C&T Publishing) are two great resources to help you brush up on your quiltmaking skills.*

Fabrics

Where do I even begin? The fabric lover in me wants to tell you to buy them all—whatever you like. Go crazy. However, the practical side (a.k.a. the husband) says, "No way!" So, where do you start?

PRECUT FABRICS

Precuts take all the guesswork out of choosing fabrics. If you've heard of precuts but aren't quite sure what they are, here's the lowdown.

Precuts are various sizes of conveniently bundled, coordinating fabrics. These little bundles of fabric goodness are a great way to purchase all or most of the fabrics from one fabric line without going broke or getting kicked out of the house. The great thing about precuts, aside from their handy size, is that you have an instant fabric collection of coordinating fabrics.

So, what sizes are these fabrics cut into? My go-to precuts are as follows:

5" × 5" Squares

A precut pack of fabric consisting of 5" × 5" squares of fabric is often called a charm pack, a 5" stacker, or charm squares. The number of squares included will vary from around 20 to 40 squares, depending on the line of fabric and fabric manufacturer.

Precut fabrics

10″ × 10″ Squares

I find that I use these squares more often than any other precut. Usually called layer cakes, 10″ stackers, or 10″ squares, they feature 10″ × 10″ squares of fabric from one fabric line. The number of squares included will vary just like the 5″ × 5″ precuts but is usually about 20–40 squares, depending on the fabric line and fabric manufacturer.

2½″ Strips

These cute little fabric rolls consist of 2½″ × width of fabric strips from one line of fabric. You will find these called jelly rolls, rolie polies, roll ups, or design rolls. The number of strips in each roll will vary from about 20 to 40, depending on the fabric line and fabric manufacturer.

Fat Quarter Bundles

The big daddy of them all—the fat quarter bundle. Fat quarter bundles were the first specialty precuts of fabric on the market and still remain one of the most popular. A fat quarter bundle consists of coordinating fat quarters (18″ × 22″) of fabric, usually from one fabric line. The number of fat quarters in a bundle varies. Bundles from the manufacturer typically include most of the fabrics within a line. Quilt shop owners often sell their own customized fat quarter bundles. Many times these bundles include an assortment of fabrics from multiple fabric lines. Custom quilt shop bundles are a great way to pick up coordinating fabrics from several fabric lines.

Fat Eighth Bundles

A fat eighth bundle could be considered the fat quarter bundle's little sister. If you purchase a fat eighth bundle, you will receive one fat eighth cut (9″ × 22″) of each of several coordinating fabrics from one fabric line. The number of fabrics included varies but typically will include most, if not all, of the fabrics from one line of fabric.

Not only are precuts handy (and fun to look at—I may have been known to have a few stacked around my house as decor), they also work beautifully in projects. For projects that require a scrappy mix of coordinating fabrics, precuts might be your best friend. You will find both fabric yardages and the precut equivalents listed in the yardage requirements throughout this book.

I love the convenience of precut fabrics, but I also enjoy mixing and matching from various collections. When choosing fabrics to add to your stash for use in appliqué, I have a few tips.

OTHER FABRICS

You don't have to stick to precuts for the quilts in this book. You may already have a good fabric stash or want to add to the fabrics you have. Here are some suggestions on the types of fabric to look for.

Scale

Fabric scale refers to the pattern or print size of any given fabric. When you are choosing fabrics for appliqué, the scale size should be proportionate to the appliqué piece size. *Tossed Petals* (page 62) is a great example of how appliqué showcases small-scale fabrics.

Now, if you are like me, there are some large, fun prints that you just can't pass up. Go ahead and buy them! These prints will work great in quilts such as or *Daisy Fields* (page 54) or *Flower Garden* (page 70).

Basics and Blenders

Fabric designers often include a variety of fabric basics or blenders within each of their collections. These are fabrics with fewer colors and a simple design aesthetic—think polka dots, stripes, or small geometric prints. While you may be drawn to the flashier prints in a collection, don't underestimate the less "exciting" fabrics within a line of fabric. They often play well with other fabric collections, and you may be surprised at how well they can stand alone.

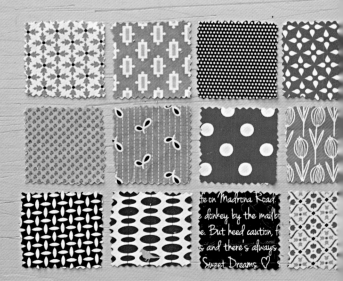

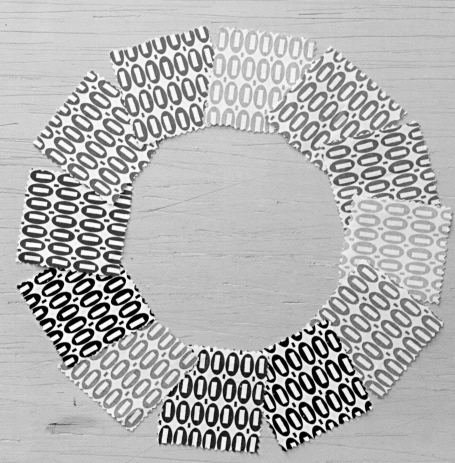

Solids also fit into this category. *Posey Patch* (page 102) shows just what visual impact a quilt full of basics can have. It is a great idea to have a wide variety of solids in your stash.

How Much Fabric to Buy

Because fabrics come and go so quickly, I much prefer to buy when the fabrics are readily available. Often, this means I am buying to add to my stash instead of buying for a specific project. I tend to buy in smaller amounts—either fat quarters or 1/3-yard cuts of fabric. If I really see myself using a lot of the fabric, I might purchase 1/2 yard. I also tend to buy great basics in multiple colors.

tip

If you have a light-color appliqué and a background that is a dark fabric or a busy print, the background may shadow or show through the appliqué. Using a lighter background fabric, darker appliqué pieces, or both will eliminate this problem.

THE GREAT PREWASH DEBATE

There is an ongoing debate about the necessity of prewashing fabrics prior to using them in a quilt. When I began making quilts about fifteen years ago, I prewashed everything. As I became more familiar with my likes and dislikes and began working with fabric more, I stopped prewashing, and now I rarely prewash any fabrics. However, there are a few guidelines I always follow:

- I always use a Color Catcher (by Shout) the first time or two that I wash a quilt. Sometimes I throw in two Color Catchers—especially if my quilt has a lot of bright colors and a white background.
- I always work with high-quality quilt shop fabrics.
- If I am going to appliqué onto clothing, I prewash *all* the fabrics and clothing items.

Following these guidelines, I have never had a problem with my choice to not prewash my fabrics. That said, as I mentioned earlier, I have never had a problem with fusible web not adhering properly to fabric that is not prewashed. This can sometimes occur and is certainly something to keep in mind if you opt to not prewash your fabrics.

Finish It!

You have completed a quilt top or pillow top, so what now? Don't let it become a UFO (unfinished object) when you can have a finished project to show off in no time.

QUILT FINISHING

Backing

To complete the backing for the quilt, follow the cutting instructions included in the project instructions. Remove the selvages, place the fabric right sides together, and sew. Press the seam to one side or open as preferred. Pressing the backing seams open minimizes seam bulk. In addition, using a ½″ seam allowance for backing seams lends added stability.

> *tip*   *For some reason, making quilt backings is one of my least favorite quiltmaking tasks. I have found that if I complete the backing at the beginning of my project, I feel like I am one step ahead of the game when it comes time for the quilting.*

NOTE

If you are machine or hand quilting, the backing and batting should be 2″ larger on all sides than the quilt top. If you are sending your quilt top out to be professionally machine quilted, the backing and batting should be 4″ larger on all sides than the quilt top—*but* be sure to check with your quilter before preparing the quilt back. The backing instructions in this book allow at least an additional 4″ on each side. For smaller projects, 2″ on all sides is adequate.

Batting

I always choose a low-loft batting. My choice of cotton or polyester batting varies. Polyester can be a bit friendlier for hand quilting and tends to be lighter weight. It does not need to be quilted as densely as cotton batting. Cotton batting, if not prewashed, will shrink slightly when washed and dried, giving your quilt that lovely vintage crinkly look.

If you are sending your quilt out to be quilted, most longarm quilters will have their preferred batting on hand to use for your quilt.

Making a Quilt Sandwich

Making a quilt sandwich is simply the process of layering your quilt top, batting, and backing and basting them together in preparation for quilting.

NOTE

If you are sending your quilt top to a machine quilter, you don't need to make the quilt sandwich—just take (or send) the quilt top and backing to the quilter.

If you are hand quilting and have a quilt frame, you'll need to make the quilt sandwich, but you can skip the safety pin basting (Step 4, at right); otherwise, pin baste it and then quilt in a large hoop.

Important: If you plan on marking the quilting lines, do so prior to layering and basting. I use a water-soluble marker to mark my quilt tops.

1. Place the quilt backing wrong side up on a clean, flat surface such as a large table or open floor space. Use masking tape to secure the backing to the surface. The backing should be taut but not stretched.

2. Place the quilt batting in the center of the backing. Gently smooth out all the wrinkles.

3. Place the quilt top, centered, on top of the batting. Smooth out the wrinkles and make sure the edges of the quilt top run parallel to the edges of the backing.

4. Starting in the center of the quilt sandwich, use safety pins (curved if possible) to baste the 3 layers together. Safety pins should be no further than 5″ apart, completely covering the quilt top.

Quilting

Quilts can be quilted by machine or by hand. To quilt by machine, use a walking foot for straight-line quilting and either a darning foot or free-motion foot for free-motion work. If you need some tips or guidance along the way, two excellent resources for machine quilting are *Beginner's Guide to Free-Motion Quilting* by Natalia Bonner or *Free-Motion Quilting with Angela Walters* (both from C&T Publishing).

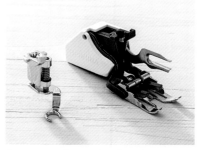

Free-motion foot and walking foot

I love the visual interest that long-stitch or pick-stitch hand quilting adds to a quilt. I prefer to use colorful perle cotton size 8. Because the thread is thicker than traditional quilting thread and I take longer stitches, I use an embroidery needle for hand quilting. Don't forget your thimble!

Perle cotton threads

> *tip*   *If your thimble is causing you to feel all thumbs, try another! That thick silver thimble your grandma used might not be the thimble for you. Now you can try rubber thimbles, leather thimbles, or thimble pads.*

Sunshine and Clouds
pillow (page 98)

Rainbow Petals
detail (page 38)

Binding

Trim excess batting and backing from the quilt, even with the quilt top. I like to use a double-fold straight-grain binding as described below.

1. Cut binding strips at 2¼″ × width of fabric and piece them together with diagonal seams to make a continuous binding strip. Trim the seam allowance to ¼″. Press the seams open.

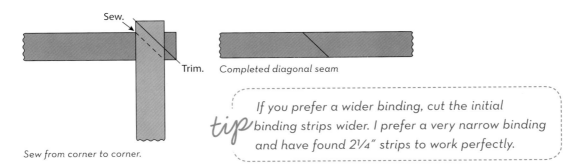

Sew from corner to corner.

Completed diagonal seam

tip If you prefer a wider binding, cut the initial binding strips wider. I prefer a very narrow binding and have found 2¼″ strips to work perfectly.

2. Press the entire strip in half lengthwise with wrong sides together. With the raw edges even, pin the binding to the front edge of the quilt a few inches away from a corner, leaving the first few inches of the binding unattached. Start sewing, using a ¼″ seam allowance.

3. Stop ¼″ away from the first corner (A) and backstitch a stitch. Lift the presser foot and needle. Rotate the quilt a quarter-turn. Fold the binding at a right angle so it extends straight above the quilt and the fold forms a 45° angle in the corner (B). Then bring the binding strip down even with the edge of the quilt (C). Begin sewing at the folded edge.

Repeat in the same manner at all corners.

End stitching ¼″ from corner.

A. *Stitch to ¼″ from corner.*

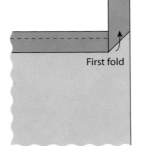

First fold

B. *First fold for miter*

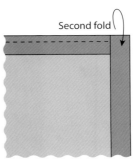

Second fold

C. *Second fold alignment*

4. Continue stitching until you are near the beginning of the binding strip.

5. Fold the ending tail of the binding back on itself where it meets the beginning binding tail. From the fold, measure and mark the cut width of the binding strip. Cut the ending binding tail to this measurement. For example, if the binding is cut 2¼″ wide, measure from the fold on the ending tail of the binding 2¼″ and cut the binding tail to this length.

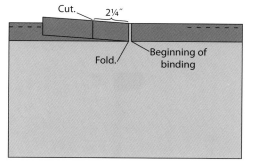

Cut binding tail.

6. Open both tails. Place one tail on top of the other tail at right angles, right sides together. Mark a diagonal line from corner to corner and stitch on the line. Check that you've done it correctly and that the binding fits the quilt; then trim the seam allowance to ¼″. Press open.

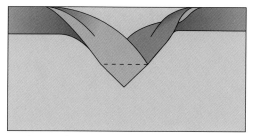

Stitch ends of binding diagonally.

7. Refold the binding and stitch this binding section in place on the quilt. Fold the binding over the raw edges to the quilt back and hand stitch.

PILLOW FINISHING

Finishing a pillow is very similar to finishing a quilt. The main difference between the two is the addition of an envelope enclosure on the back of the pillow.

Making a Pillow Top Sandwich

Refer to Making a Quilt Sandwich (page 29) as needed.

The pillow top sandwich consists of three layers: the pillow top, the batting (page 29), and a piece of muslin for the back. These layers can be safety pin basted (page 29) or basted using a temporary fabric spray adhesive (this is always my personal choice for pillows and very small quilts).

Quilting the Pillow Top

Refer to Quilting (page 30) as needed.

Pillows are a great way to try out new quilting techniques. If you have always wanted to try hand quilting or machine quilting, now is the time to give it a whirl!

Pillow Back

Add the pillow back after the pillow top has been quilted.

1. Cut the 2 backing rectangles as indicated in the instructions for each pillow.

2. Hem a long side of each rectangle. For example, if the instructions say to cut 2 rectangles 12½″ × 18½″, hem an

18½″ side on each rectangle. To hem the rectangle, place the rectangular fabric wrong side up, fold over the longer edge ¼″, and press. Fold over the edge an additional ¼″ and press again. Sew the edge down.

3. Align the backing pieces with the back of the pillow top. The backing should be *right side up*, with the raw edges aligned with the raw edges of the pillow top and the hemmed edges of the backing pieces overlapping in the center.

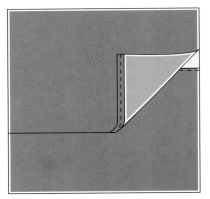

Align backing.

4. Pin the backing in place and machine baste approximately ⅛″ from the pillow edge.

Binding a Pillow

Bind the pillow as you would a quilt (page 32).

Pillow Back
Cutting Guide

This handy guide includes the cutting dimensions for a number of standard pillow sizes.

Finished pillow size:	Cut 2 rectangles:
12" × 12"	12½" × 9½"
14" × 14"	14½" × 10½"
16" × 16"	16½" × 11½"
18" × 18"	18½" × 12½"
20" × 20"	20½" × 13½"
22" × 22"	22½" × 14½"
24" × 24"	24½" × 15½"
12" × 16"	16½" × 9½"

Projects

Rainbow Petals Quilt

Finished quilt: 48½" × 60½" *Finished block:* 8" × 12"

Fabrics: Simply Color by Vanessa Christenson, Cuzco by Kate Spain, and Sew Stitchy by Aneela Hoey, all for Moda Fabrics

Pieced by Corey Yoder • Quilted by Jody Hershberger

Materials

- ⅛ yard each of 25 different prints or 38 precut 10″ × 10″ squares (layer cake) for petals

- 3 yards fabric for background and sashing

- ½ yard fabric for binding

- 3¼ yards fabric for backing

- 3½ yards fusible web (based on 17″ width)

- 56″ × 68″ piece of batting

Cutting Instructions

From background and sashing fabric:

- Cut 9 strips 8½″ × width of fabric; subcut into 25 rectangles 8½″ × 12½″.

- Cut 7 strips 2½″ × width of fabric, trim the selvages, sew end to end, press the seams open, and cut 4 strips 2½″ × 60½″.

From binding fabric:

- Cut 6 strips 2¼″ × width of fabric and continue as instructed in Binding (page 32).

From backing fabric:

- Cut 2 pieces 57″ × width of fabric. Sew together the pieces to form a horizontal seam in the backing.

tip *Make the binding and the backing for the quilt right after cutting all the quilt top pieces. Then when the quilt top is finished, you can dive right into quilting it or send it off to your quilter. And after it's quilted, the binding will be ready to go.*

Petal Construction

Refer to Appliqué Basics (page 8) as needed.

1. Use the petal pattern (page 43) to trace 150 petals onto the fusible web. Use the petal placement guide (page 10) for optimal petal placement.

2. Cut out the petals and trim the interior of each petal (page 10).

3. Fuse the petals to the wrong side of the fabrics: 6 petals per ⅛ yard or 4 petals per 10″ square.

4. Cut out the fabric petals, remove the paper backing, and set them aside.

Block Construction

Note: All sewing is done right sides together with a ¼″ seam allowance, unless otherwise noted.

Lightly finger-press each rectangle in half lengthwise to mark the center.

Adding the Appliqué

1. For each block, fuse 3 pairs of petals an equal distance apart. Use the creased centerline to help with placement. Allow a ¼″ seam allowance around the perimeter of the block.

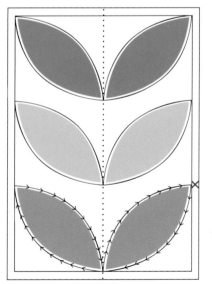

Petal placement and appliqué stitching guide

2. Finish the appliqué edges as desired (pages 12–16). Begin and end the stitching at the X. Stitch the outer edges and then the inner edges of each pair. Make 25 blocks 8½″ × 12½″.

Quilt Top Assembly

1. Sew together the blocks into 5 columns of 5 blocks each. Press the seams in one direction.

2. Join together the columns with the 2½″ × 60½″ sashing strips. Press the seams away from the sashing strips.

Quilt assembly diagram

Finishing It

Refer to Quilt Finishing (pages 28–33) as needed.

1. Layer the backing, the batting, and the quilt top. Baste and quilt as desired.

2. Trim the excess batting and backing from the quilt and bind.

Why not dive headfirst into appliqué with this colorful quilt? Choose fabrics with a wide range of colors for a rainbow effect or just go scrappy. After stitching all the appliqué featured on this quilt, you will certainly be an appliqué pro!

Rainbow Petals Pillow

Finished pillow: 16" × 12"   *Finished block:* 8" × 12"

Fabrics: Assorted fabrics from my stash

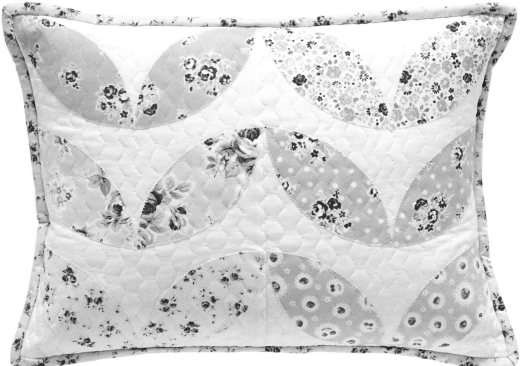

Pieced and quilted by Corey Yoder

Materials

- Scraps of 6 fabrics, ¼ yard total for petals

- ⅓ yard solid fabric for background

- ¼ yard fabric for binding

- ⅓ yard fabric for backing

- ⅓ yard fusible web (based on 17" width)

- 14" × 18" piece of batting

- 14" × 18" piece of muslin for pillow sandwich

- 12" × 16" rectangular pillow form

Cutting Instructions

From background fabric:

- Cut 2 rectangles 8½″ × 12½″.

From binding fabric:

- Cut 2 strips 2¼″ × width of fabric and continue as instructed in Binding (page 32).

From backing fabric:

- Cut 2 rectangles 9½″ × 16½″ and continue as instructed in Pillow Back (page 34).

Petal and Block Construction

1. Refer to Petal Construction (page 39). Use 12 petals in Step 1. In Step 3, fuse 2 petals to the wrong side of each of the 6 fabrics.

2. Refer to Block Construction (page 40) to make 2 blocks 8½″ × 12½″.

Adding the Appliqué

Refer to Adding the Appliqué (page 40) for fusing the petals.

Pillow Top Assembly

Sew together the 2 blocks to complete the pillow top.

Finishing It

Refer to Pillow Finishing (page 34) as needed.

1. Layer the pillow top, the batting, and the muslin.

2. Quilt as desired.

3. Layer the quilted pillow top and the 2 backing pieces. Pin in place, baste, and bind.

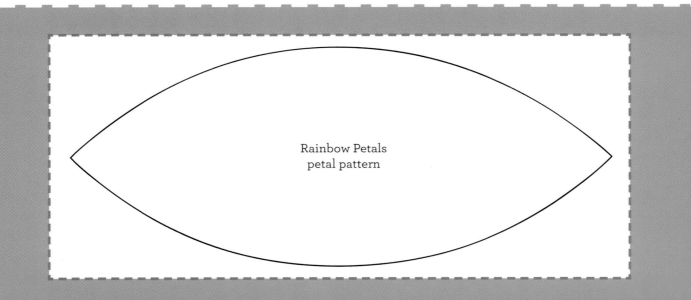

Rainbow Petals
petal pattern

Starflower Quilt

Finished quilt: 58½" × 72½"   *Finished block:* 12" × 12"

Fabrics: Mix of fabrics from my stash

Pieced by Corey Yoder   •   Quilted by Margaret Solomon Gunn

Materials

- ⅛ yard each of 20 different prints or 20 fat eighths for star points
- 4½ yards solid fabric for background and sashing
- 1¼ yards print fabric for petals and sashing squares
- ⅝ yard fabric for binding
- 3¾ yards fabric for backing
- 2½ yards fusible web (based on 17" width)
- 66" × 80" piece of batting

Cutting Instructions

From each of 20 star point fabrics:

- Cut 1 strip 3½" × width of fabric; subcut into 8 squares 3½" × 3½" and mark a diagonal line on the wrong side of each square (if you are using fat eighths, cut 8 squares 3½" × 3½" from each fat eighth and mark with diagonal lines).

From background and sashing fabric:

- Cut 14 strips 3½" × width of fabric; subcut into 80 rectangles 3½" × 6½".
- Cut 4 strips 6½" × width of fabric; subcut into 20 squares 6½" × 6½".
- Cut 8 strips 3½" × width of fabric; subcut into 80 squares 3½" × 3½".
- Cut 17 strips 2½" × width of fabric; subcut into 49 rectangles 2½" × 12½".

From petal fabric:

- Cut 2 strips 2½" × width of fabric; subcut into 30 squares 2½" × 2½". Set aside the remaining fabric for the petal construction.

From binding fabric:

- Cut 7 strips 2¼" × width of fabric and continue as instructed in Binding (page 32).

From backing fabric:

- Cut 2 pieces 67" × width of fabric. Sew together the pieces to form a horizontal seam in the backing.

Petal Construction

Refer to Appliqué Basics (page 8) as needed.

1. Use the 2 petal patterns (page 53) to trace 80 large petals and 160 small petals onto the fusible web. Use the petal placement guide (page 10) for optimal petal placement.

2. Cut out the petals and trim the interior of each petal (page 10).

3. Fuse the petals to the wrong side of the petal fabric.

4. Cut out the fabric petals, remove the paper backing, and set them aside.

Block Construction

Note: All sewing is done right sides together with a 1/4" seam allowance, unless otherwise noted.

MAKING THE STAR POINTS

1. Place a 3½" × 3½" print square right sides together with a 3½" × 6½" rectangle. Refer to illustration A for square placement and orientation.

2. Sew together the pieces on the marked line. Trim away the fabric, leaving a ¼" seam allowance. Press the seam away from the white. (Figures A and B)

3. Repeat with another 3½" × 3½" print square on the other end of the rectangle. (Figure C)

4. Repeat to make 80 units 3½" × 6½", 4 from each star point fabric. (Figure D)

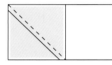
A. Place square on rectangle. Sew and trim.

B. Press.

C. Sew and trim.

D. Make 80.

ASSEMBLING THE BLOCK

1. Sew 2 matching 3½" × 6½" star point units to the sides of a 6½" × 6½" solid background square as shown. Press the seams away from the center.

2. Sew 3½" × 3½" solid background squares to the ends of the 2 remaining matching star point units. Press the seams toward the center.

3. Sew the 2 units made in Step 2 to the top and bottom of the unit made in Step 1 as shown. Press the seams away from the center.

4. Repeat with the other star point units to make a total of 20 blocks 12½" × 12½".

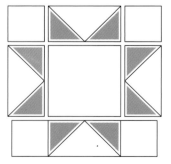
Make 20.

My favorite color changes daily; however, there is one surefire color combo that gets me every time I see it—peachy coral, aqua, green, taupe, and yellow. When I found myself repeatedly mixing and matching fabrics in these colors, I knew it was time to bring this combination to life.

Adding the Appliqué

1. Fuse 4 large petals onto the corners of each block. Allow a ¼″ seam allowance around the perimeter of the block. Place the small petals in the star points and in the center of the block as indicated.

2. Finish the appliqué edges as desired (pages 12–16). Begin and end the stitching at the center of the center petals. Stitch the outer petals individually. Begin and end the stitching at the X.

Petal placement and appliqué stitching guide

Quilt Top Assembly

1. Sew together the blocks in 5 rows of 4 blocks each, placing 2½″ × 12½″ sashing rectangles between the blocks and on the ends of each row. Press the seams away from the blocks.

2. Sew together 4 sashing rectangles 2½″ × 12½″ and 5 squares 2½″ × 2½″. Repeat to make 6 sashing rows.

3. Arrange the quilt top and sew together the completed sashing rows and the block rows.

Quilt assembly diagram

Finishing It

Refer to Quilt Finishing (pages 28–33) as needed.

1. Layer the backing, the batting, and the quilt top. Baste and quilt as desired.

2. Trim the excess batting and backing from the quilt and bind.

Starflower Pillow

Finished pillow: 18" × 18"   *Finished block:* 12" × 12"

Fabrics: Oval Elements by Art Gallery Fabrics and Secret Garden by Sandi Henderson for Michael Miller Fabrics

Pieced and quilted by Corey Yoder

Materials

- ⅛ yard print fabric for star points
- ¼ yard solid fabric for background
- ⅛ yard solid fabric for petals
- ⅛ yard print fabric for first border
- ¼ yard print fabric for second border
- ¼ yard fabric for binding
- ½ yard fabric for backing
- ¼ yard fusible web (based on 17″ width)
- 20″ × 20″ piece of batting
- 20″ × 20″ piece of muslin for pillow sandwich
- 18″ × 18″ square pillow form

Cutting Instructions

From star point fabric:

- Cut 1 strip 3½″ × width of fabric; subcut into 8 squares 3½″ × 3½″ and mark a diagonal line on the wrong side of each square.

From background fabric:

- Cut 1 square 6½″ × 6½″.
- Cut 1 strip 3½″ × remaining width of fabric; subcut into 4 rectangles 3½″ × 6½″.
- Cut 1 strip 3½″ × remaining width of fabric; subcut into 4 squares 3½″ × 3½″.

From first border fabric:

- Cut 2 strips 1½″ × width of fabric; subcut into 2 rectangles 1½″ × 12½″ and 2 rectangles 1½″ × 14½″.

From second border fabric:

- Cut 2 strips 2½″ × width of fabric; subcut into 2 rectangles 2½″ × 14½″ and 2 rectangles 2½″ × 18½″.

From binding fabric:

- Cut 2 strips 2¼″ × width of fabric and continue as instructed in Binding (page 32).

From backing fabric:

- Cut 2 rectangles 12½″ × 18½″ and continue as instructed in Pillow Back (page 34).

I enjoy trying out new quilting techniques on small projects. For this pillow I used three different quilting techniques: one for the center of the pillow, a second for the first border, and a third for the outer border. Small projects are a great way to try something out and see if you like it.

Petal and Block Construction

1. Refer to Petal Construction (page 45). Use 4 large petals and 8 small petals in Step 1.

2. Refer to Block Construction (page 46) to make 1 block 12½" × 12½".

Adding the Appliqué

Refer to Adding the Appliqué (page 48) for fusing the petals.

Pillow Top Assembly

1. Sew 1½" × 12½" border pieces to the sides of the 12½" × 12½" pillow center. Press the seams away from the center. Sew 1½" × 14½" border pieces to the top and bottom of the pillow center. Press the seams away from the center.

2. Sew 2½" × 14½" second border pieces to the left and right of the unit made in Step 1. Press the seams away from the center. Sew 2½" × 18½" border pieces to the top and bottom of the pillow. Press the seams away from the center.

Pillow assembly diagram

Finishing It

Refer to Pillow Finishing (page 34) as needed.

1. Layer the pillow top, the batting, and the muslin.

2. Quilt as desired.

3. Layer the quilted pillow top and the 2 backing pieces. Pin into place, baste, and bind.

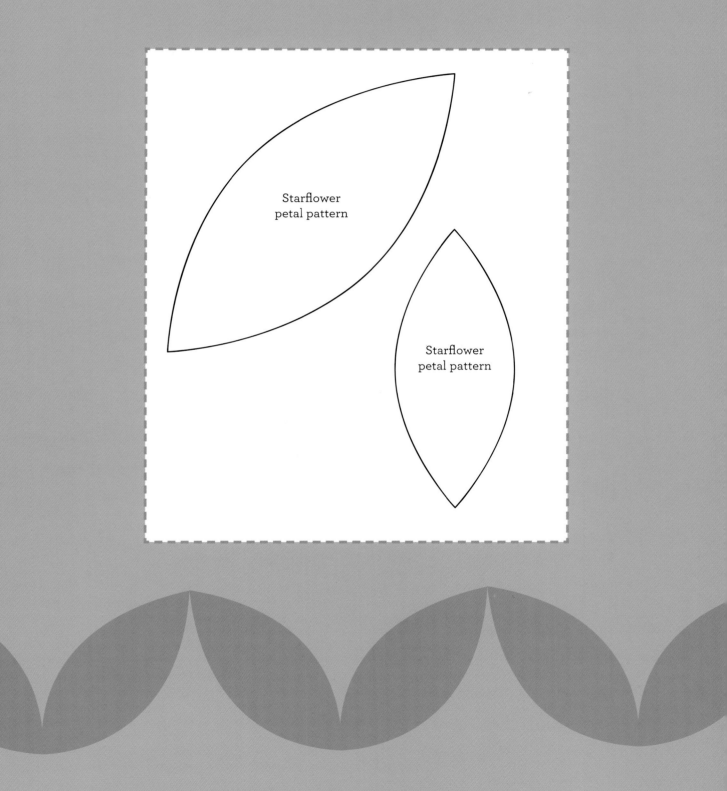

Starflower
petal pattern

Starflower
petal pattern

Daisy Fields Quilt

Finished quilt: 53½" × 64½"   *Finished block:* 9" × 9"

Fabrics: Notting Hill by Joel Dewberry for FreeSpirit Fabrics

Pieced by Corey Yoder • Quilted by Natalia Bonner

Materials

- ⅓ yard each of 10 print fabrics or 30 precut 10″ × 10″ squares (layer cake) for blocks

- 2¼ yards white solid fabric for background

- 1 yard solid fabric for petals

- ⅝ yard fabric for binding

- 3½ yards fabric for backing

- 2 yards fusible web (based on 17″ width)

- 61″ × 72″ piece of batting

Cutting Instructions

From each of 10 print fabrics:

- Cut 1 strip 9½″ × width of fabric; subcut into 3 squares 9½″ × 9½″ or, if you are using 10″ × 10″ squares, trim the 30 squares to 9½″ × 9½″.

From background fabric:

- Cut 11 strips 3½″ × width of fabric; subcut into 120 squares 3½″ × 3½″ and mark a diagonal line on the wrong side of each square.

- Cut 6 strips 2½″ × width of fabric; subcut into 24 rectangles 2½″ × 9½″.

- Cut 7 strips 2½″ × width of fabric; trim the selvages, sew end to end, press the seams open, and cut 5 strips 2½″ × 53½″.

From binding fabric:

- Cut 7 strips 2¼″ × width of fabric and continue as instructed in Binding (page 32).

From backing fabric:

- Cut 2 pieces 62″ × width of fabric. Sew together the pieces to form a horizontal seam in the backing.

Petal Construction

Refer to Appliqué Basics (page 8) as needed.

1. Use the petal pattern (page 61) to trace 160 petals onto the fusible web. Use the petal placement guide (page 10) for optimal petal placement.

2. Cut out the petals and trim the interior of each petal (page 10).

3. Fuse the petals to the wrong side of the petal fabric.

4. Cut out the fabric petals, remove the paper backing, and set them aside.

Block Construction

Note: All sewing is done right sides together with a ¼" seam allowance, unless otherwise noted.

1. Place white background squares on the corners of a large print square. Refer to the illustration for square placement and orientation.

2. Sew on the traced line. Trim the excess fabric, leaving a ¼" seam allowance. Press the seams away from the center.

3. Repeat to make 30 blocks 9½" × 9½".

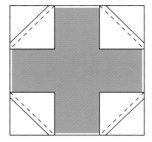

Make 30.

Quilt Top Assembly, Part 1

Important! This quilt top is constructed by assembling 2 rows, completing the appliqué, and then adding more rows.

1. Sew together the blocks in 6 rows of 5 blocks each, placing 2½" × 9½" sashing rectangles between the blocks. Press the seams away from the blocks.

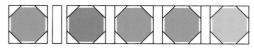

Make 6.

2. Sew together the top 2 rows of the quilt, placing a 2½" × 53½" sashing strip between them. Press the seams away from the blocks.

Adding the Appliqué

1. Center and fuse 8 petals onto the open spaces created by the sashing and blocks.

Petal placement

2. Finish the appliqué edges as desired (pages 12–16). Stitch each petal individually. Begin and end the stitching at the points in the center. See the stitching guide for the pillow (page 60).

Bright splashy prints against a sea of white equal perfection in my book! This quilt is perfect for showing off those larger prints you've been waiting to use. Be careful when choosing the petal fabric, as the chosen color will definitely set the tone of the quilt.

Quilt Top Assembly, Part 2

1. Sew a third row of the quilt onto the unit just completed. Place a 2½″ × 53½″ sashing strip between the second and third rows. Press the seams away from the blocks.

2. Fuse 4 more sets of petals as indicated in Adding the Appliqué (page 56). Set this section of rows aside.

3. Repeat Quilt Top Assembly, Part 1 and Quilt Top Assembly, Part 2 (Steps 1 and 2) to sew together and add the petals to the remaining 3 rows.

4. Sew together the 2 sets of 3 rows, placing a 2½″ × 53½″ sashing strip between them. Press the seams away from the blocks.

5. Complete the appliqué.

Finishing It

Refer to Quilt Finishing (pages 28–33) as needed.

1. Layer the backing, the batting, and the quilt top. Baste and quilt as desired.

2. Trim the excess batting and backing from the quilt and bind.

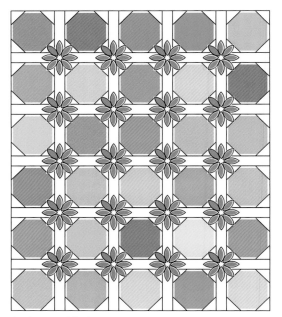

Quilt assembly diagram

Daisy Fields Pillow

Finished pillow: 14" × 14"   *Finished block:* 9" × 9"

Fabrics: Cold Spring Dream by Mary McGuire for RJR Fabrics

Pieced and quilted by Corey Yoder

Materials

- 9½" × 9½" print square for block center
- ⅛ yard solid fabric for corners
- ⅛ yard fabric for first border
- ¼ yard fabric for second border
- ¼ yard fabric for binding
- ½ yard fabric for backing
- ¼ yard fusible web (based on 17" width)
- 16" × 16" piece of batting
- 16" × 16" piece of muslin for pillow sandwich
- 14" × 14" square pillow form

Cutting Instructions

From solid fabric:

- Cut 1 strip 3½" × width of fabric; subcut into 4 squares 3½" × 3½" and mark a diagonal line on the wrong side of each square.

From first border fabric:

- Cut 1 strip 1" × width of fabric; subcut into 2 rectangles 1" × 9½" and 2 rectangles 1" × 10½".

From second border fabric:

- Cut 2 strips 2½" × width of fabric; subcut into 2 rectangles 2½" × 10½" and 2 rectangles 2½" × 14½".

From binding fabric:

- Cut 2 strips 2¼" × width of fabric and continue as instructed in Binding (page 32).

From backing fabric:

- Cut 2 rectangles 10½" × 14½" and continue as instructed in Pillow Back (page 34).

Petal and Block Construction

1. Refer to Petal Construction (page 55). Use 8 petals.

2. Refer to Block Construction (page 56) to make 1 block 9½" × 9½".

Adding the Appliqué

1. Center and fuse the 8 petals onto the block.

Petal placement and appliqué stitching guide

2. Finish the appliqué edges as desired (pages 12–16). Stitch each petal individually. Begin and end the stitching at the X.

Pillow Top Assembly

1. Sew 1" × 9½" border pieces to the sides of the 9½" × 9½" pillow center. Press the seams away from the center. Sew 1" × 10½" border pieces to the top and bottom of the pillow center. Press the seams away from the center.

2. Sew 2½" × 10½" second border pieces to the sides of the unit made in Step 1. Press the seams away from the center. Sew 2½" × 14½" border pieces to the top and bottom of the pillow. Press the seams away from the center.

Add borders.

For the Daisy Fields pillow, the petals are placed directly onto the block instead of in the sashing as with the quilt. This is a great way to change up the look of the block while using the same basic technique.

Finishing It

Refer to Pillow Finishing (page 34) as needed.

1. Layer the pillow top, the batting, and the muslin.

2. Quilt as desired.

3. Layer the quilted pillow top and 2 backing pieces. Pin into place, baste, and bind.

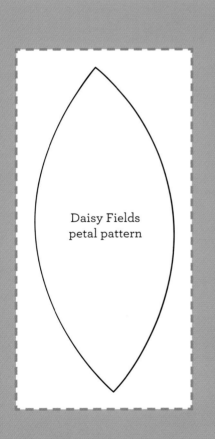

Daisy Fields petal pattern

Tossed Petals Quilt

Finished quilt: 48½" × 60½"   *Finished block:* 12" × 12"

Fabrics: From various collections by Moda Fabrics and Riley Blake Designs

Pieced by Corey Yoder • Quilted by Natalia Bonner

Materials

- ⅛ yard each of 14 different prints or 70 precut 5″ × 5″ squares (charm squares) for petals

- 1⅓ yards dark gray solid fabric for pieced blocks

- 2¼ yards white solid fabric for pieced blocks

- ½ yard fabric for binding

- 3¼ yards fabric for backing

- 2 yards fusible web (based on 17″ width)

- 56″ × 68″ piece of batting

Cutting Instructions

From dark gray solid fabric:

- Cut 4 strips 3½″ × width of fabric; subcut into 40 squares 3½″ × 3½″.

- Cut 7 strips 3½″ × width of fabric; subcut into 40 rectangles 3½″ × 6½″.

From white solid fabric:

- Cut 4 strips 6½″ × width of fabric; subcut into 20 squares 6½″ × 6½″.

- Cut 4 strips 3½″ × width of fabric; subcut into 40 squares 3½″ × 3½″.

- Cut 7 strips 3½″ × width of fabric; subcut into 40 rectangles 3½″ × 6½″.

From binding fabric:

- Cut 6 strips 2¼″ × width of fabric and continue as instructed in Binding (page 32).

  Note: For a scrappy binding, cut each of the 6 binding strips from a different fabric.

From backing fabric:

- Cut 2 pieces 57″ × width of fabric. Sew together the pieces to form a horizontal seam in the backing.

Petal Construction

Refer to Appliqué Basics (page 8) as needed.

1. Use the petal pattern (page 69) to trace 140 petals onto the fusible web. Use the petal placement guide (page 10) for optimal petal placement.

2. Cut out the petals and trim the interior of each petal (page 10).

3. Fuse the petals onto the wrong side of the fabrics: 10 petals per ⅛ yard petal fabric or 2 petals per 5″ × 5″ precut square.

4. Cut out the fabric petals, remove the paper backing, and set them aside.

Block Construction

Note: All sewing is done right sides together with a ¼" seam allowance, unless otherwise noted.

BLOCK 1

1. Sew 3½" × 6½" gray rectangles to the sides of 10 of the 6½" × 6½" squares. Press the seams away from the center.

2. Sew 3½" × 3½" white squares to the ends of each of the remaining 20 gray 3½" × 6½" rectangles. Press the seams toward the gray fabric.

3. Sew 2 units made in Step 2 to the top and bottom of a unit made in Step 1. Press the seams away from the center.

4. Repeat Steps 1–3 to make 10 blocks 12½" × 12½".

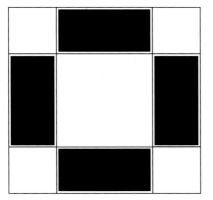

Make 10.

BLOCK 2

1. Sew 3½" × 6½" white rectangles to the sides of 10 of the 6½" × 6½" squares. Press the seams toward the center.

2. Sew 3½" × 3½" gray squares to the sides of each of the remaining 20 white 3½" × 6½" rectangles. Press the seams toward the gray fabric.

3. Sew 2 units made in Step 2 to the top and bottom of a unit made in Step 1. Press the seams toward the center.

4. Repeat Steps 1–3 to make 10 blocks 12½" × 12½".

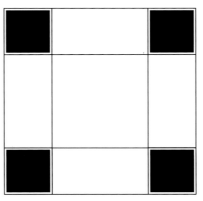

Make 10.

Interlocking petals, red and aqua flower fabrics, and some text fabrics thrown in for good measure ... what more could you want? Use charm squares for a scrappier version.

Adding the Appliqué

1. Fuse 7 petals onto each block. If you are using precut squares, spread the fabrics randomly. The petals placed in the rectangle patches should have the outer point centered on the rectangle. Allow a ¼" seam allowance around the perimeter of the block.

Petal placement and appliqué stitching guide

2. Finish the appliqué edges as desired (pages 12–16). Begin and end the stitching at the X. Each line of stitching forms a partial circle.

Quilt Top Assembly

1. Sew together the blocks in 5 rows of 4 blocks each, beginning with Block 1 in the upper left corner and alternating with Block 2. The second row will begin with Block 2, the third row with Block 1, and so on. Rotate the blocks randomly within the quilt. Press the seams in adjoining rows in opposite directions.

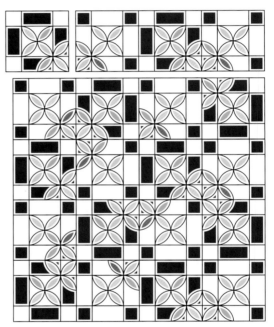

Quilt assembly diagram

2. Sew together the rows. Press the seams in one direction.

Finishing It

Refer to Quilt Finishing (pages 28–33) as needed.

1. Layer the backing, the batting, and the quilt top. Baste and quilt as desired.

2. Trim the excess batting and backing from the quilt and bind.

Tossed Petals Pillow

Finished pillow: 18″ × 18″   *Finished block:* 12″ × 12″

Fabrics: The Birds and the Bees by Tula Pink for FreeSpirit Fabrics, Mama Said Sew by Sweetwater for Moda Fabrics, and Lark by Amy Butler for Westminster Fabrics

Pieced and quilted by Corey Yoder

Materials

- Scraps for petals

- ¼ yard text fabric for background

- ⅛ yard solid fabric for corner squares

- ⅛ yard solid fabric for first border

- ¼ yard print fabric for second border

- ¼ yard fabric for binding

- ½ yard fabric for backing

- ¼ yard fusible web (based on 17″ width)

- 20″ × 20″ piece of batting

- 20″ × 20″ piece of muslin for pillow sandwich

- 18″ × 18″ square pillow form

Cutting Instructions

From background fabric:

- Cut 1 square 6½" × 6½".

- Cut 1 strip 3½" × remaining width of fabric; subcut into 4 rectangles 3½" × 6½".

Note: If you are using a directional print, you may want to cut the fabric accordingly.

From solid corner fabric:

- Cut 4 squares 3½" × 3½".

From first border fabric:

- Cut 2 strips 1½" × width of fabric; subcut into 2 rectangles 1½" × 12½" and 2 rectangles 1½" × 14½".

From second border fabric:

- Cut 2 strips 2½" × width of fabric; subcut into 2 rectangles 2½" × 14½" and 2 rectangles 2½" × 18½".

From binding fabric:

- Cut 2 strips 2¼" × width of fabric and continue as instructed in Binding (page 32).

From backing fabric:

- Cut 2 rectangles 12½" × 18½" and continue as instructed in Pillow Back (page 34).

Petal and Block Construction

1. Refer to Petal Construction (page 63). Use 7 petals.

2. Refer to Block Construction, Block 2 (page 64) to make 1 block 12½" × 12½".

Adding the Appliqué

Refer to Adding the Appliqué (page 66) for fusing the petals.

Pillow Top Assembly

1. Sew 1½" × 12½" border pieces to the top and bottom of the 12½" × 12½" pillow center. Press the seams away from the center. Sew 1½" × 14½" border pieces to the sides of the pillow center. Press the seams away from the center.

2. Sew 2½" × 14½" second border pieces to the top and bottom of the unit made in Step 1. Press the seams away from the center. Sew 2½" × 18½" border pieces to the sides of the pillow. Press the seams away from the center.

Add borders.

Finishing It

Refer to Pillow Finishing (page 34) as needed.

1. Layer the pillow top, the batting, and the muslin.

2. Quilt as desired.

3. Layer the quilted pillow top and 2 backing pieces. Pin into place, baste, and bind.

A fun text background sets off the colorful interlocking petals.

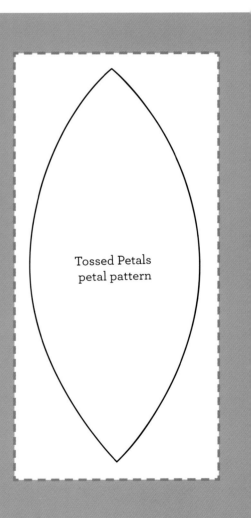

Tossed Petals petal pattern

Flower Garden Quilt

Finished quilt: 58½" × 72½"   *Finished block:* 12" × 12"

Fabrics: Happy Go Lucky by Bonnie & Camille for Moda Fabrics

Pieced by Corey Yoder • Quilted by Angela Walters

Materials

- ¼ yard each of 10 different prints or 20 precut 10″ × 10″ squares (layer cake) for block centers

- 1½ yards solid fabric for pieced blocks, sashing squares, and petals

- 2⅔ yards solid fabric for background and sashing

- ½ yard fabric for binding

- 3¾ yards fabric for backing

- 1⅔ yards fusible web (based on 17″ width)

- 66″ × 80″ piece of batting

Cutting Instructions

From each of 10 print fabrics:

- Cut 2 squares 8½″ × 8½″ or, if you are using precut squares, trim them to 8½″ × 8½″.

From solid petal fabric:

- Cut 7 strips 2½″ × width of fabric; subcut into 110 squares 2½″ × 2½″.

  Set aside the remaining fabric for the petal construction.

From solid background fabric:

- Cut 20 strips 2½″ × width of fabric; subcut into 80 rectangles 2½″ × 8½″ for the blocks.

- Cut 17 strips 2½″ × width of fabric; subcut into 49 rectangles 2½″ × 12½″ for the sashing.

From binding fabric:

- Cut 7 strips 2¼″ × width of fabric and continue as instructed in Binding (page 32).

From backing fabric:

- Cut 2 pieces 67″ × width of fabric. Sew together the pieces to form a horizontal seam in the backing.

Petal Construction

Refer to Appliqué Basics (page 8) as needed.

1. Use the petal pattern (page 76) to trace 98 petals onto the fusible web. Use the petal placement guide (page 10) for optimal petal placement.

2. Cut out the petals and trim the interior of each petal (page 10).

3. Fuse the petals to the wrong side of the petal fabric.

4. Cut out the fabric petals, remove the paper backing, and set them aside.

Block Construction

Note: All sewing is done right sides together with a ¼″ seam allowance, unless otherwise noted.

1. Sew 2½″ × 8½″ background rectangles to the sides of each 8½″ × 8½″ center square. Press the seams toward the center. Make a total of 20 units.

2. Sew 2½″ × 2½″ solid squares to the ends of each remaining 2½″ × 8½″ rectangle. Press the seams toward the squares. Make a total of 40 units.

3. Sew 2 units made in Step 2 to the top and bottom of a unit made in Step 1. Press the seams toward the center. Repeat to make 20 blocks 12½″ × 12½″.

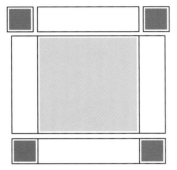

Make 20.

Adding the Appliqué

1. Fuse 2 petals onto each 2½″ × 12½″ sashing rectangle. The petals should be centered within the rectangle. Make 80 sashing pieces.

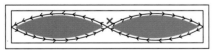

Petal placement and appliqué stitching guide

2. Finish the appliqué edges as desired (pages 12–16). Begin and end the stitching at the X.

Quilt Top Assembly

1. Sew together the blocks in 5 rows of 4 blocks each, placing sashing rectangles between the blocks and on the ends of the rows. Press the seams toward the blocks.

2. Sew together 4 sashing rectangles and 5 squares 2½″ × 2½″. Press the seams toward the squares. Repeat to make 6 sashing rows.

3. Arrange the quilt top and sew together the completed sashing rows and the block rows.

Finishing It

Refer to Quilt Finishing (pages 28–33) as needed.

1. Layer the backing, the batting, and the quilt top. Baste and quilt as desired.

2. Trim the excess batting and backing from the quilt and bind.

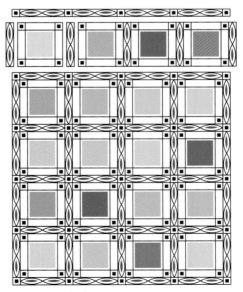

Quilt assembly diagram

In this quilt, the petals form a perfect frame around all your favorite fabrics. This is a wonderful way to draw attention to each fabric within the quilt. Work with fabrics from your stash or use precut squares to create an eye-catching quilt.

Flower Garden Pillow

Finished pillow: 16" × 16"   *Finished block:* 12" × 12"

Fabrics: Lush by Erin Michael and Sunkissed by Sweetwater, both for Moda Fabrics

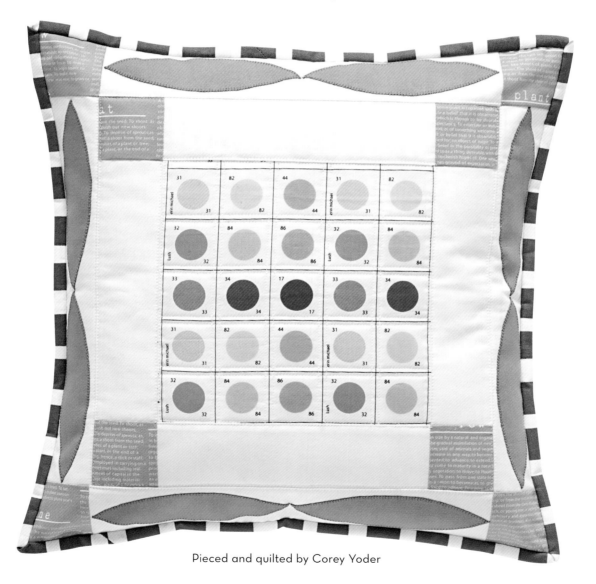

Pieced and quilted by Corey Yoder

Materials

- 8½″ × 8½″ square piece of print fabric for pillow center
- ¼ yard solid fabric for background
- ⅛ yard print fabric for corner squares
- ⅛ yard solid fabric for petals
- ¼ yard fabric for binding
- ½ yard fabric for backing
- ¼ yard fusible web (based on 17″ width)
- 18″ × 18″ piece of batting
- 18″ × 18″ piece of muslin for pillow sandwich
- 16″ × 16″ square pillow form

Cutting Instructions

From background fabric:

- Cut 1 strip 2½″ × width of fabric; subcut into 4 rectangles 2½″ × 8½″.
- Cut 2 strips 2½″ × width of fabric; subcut into 4 rectangles 2½″ × 12½″.

From corner square fabric:

- Cut 8 squares 2½″ × 2½″.

From binding fabric:

- Cut 2 strips 2¼″ × width of fabric and continue as instructed in Binding (page 32).

From backing fabric:

- Cut 2 rectangles 11½″ × 16½″ and continue as instructed in Pillow Back (page 34).

Petal and Block Construction

1. Refer to Petal Construction (page 71). Use 8 petals in Step 1.

2. Refer to Block Construction (page 71) to make 1 block 12½″ × 12½″.

Adding the Appliqué

Refer to Adding the Appliqué (page 72) for fusing the petals. Make a total of 4 petal pieces.

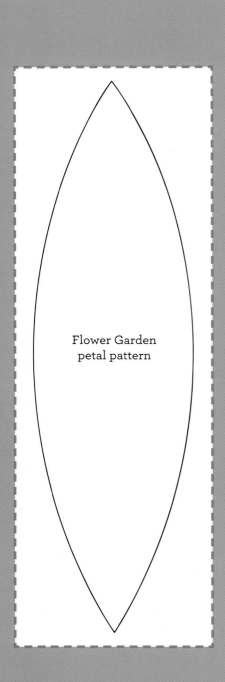

Flower Garden
petal pattern

Pillow Top Assembly

1. Sew petal pieces to the sides of the 12½″ × 12½″ block. Press the seams toward the center.

2. Sew 2½″ × 2½″ print squares to the ends of the 2 remaining petal pieces. Press the seams toward the squares.

3. Sew the units made in Step 2 to the top and bottom of the unit made in Step 1. Press the seams toward the center.

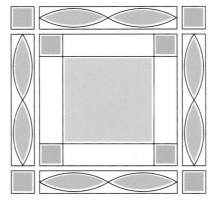

Pillow layout diagram

Finishing It

Refer to Pillow Finishing (page 34) as needed.

1. Layer the pillow top, the batting, and the muslin.

2. Quilt as desired.

3. Layer the quilted pillow top and 2 backing pieces. Pin into place, baste, and bind.

I decided to fussy cut a bit of fabric I have been hoarding in my fabric stash for years. This is the perfect design to showcase a favorite fabric.

Scattered Blossoms Quilt

Finished quilt: 48½" × 60½"   *Finished block:* 12" × 12"

Fabrics: Petal fabrics are a mix of scrap fabrics from my never-ending scrap bin.

Pieced by Corey Yoder • Quilted by Natalia Bonner

Materials

- A variety of fabric scraps or 80 precut 5″ × 5″ squares (charm squares) for petals

- 1½ yards light solid fabric for background

- 2 yards medium-light solid fabric for background

- ½ yard fabric for binding

- 3¼ yards fabric for backing

- 2¼ yards fusible web (based on 17″ width)

- 56″ × 68″ piece of batting

Cutting Instructions

From light solid background fabric:

- Cut 10 strips 4¾″ × width of fabric; subcut into 80 squares 4¾″ × 4¾″.

From medium-light solid background fabric:

- Cut 3 strips 4¾″ × width of fabric; subcut into 20 squares 4¾″ × 4¾″.

- Cut 4 strips 7¼″ × width of fabric; subcut into 20 squares 7¼″ × 7¼″ and cut each square diagonally twice to form 80 large triangles.

- Cut 4 strips 3⅞″ × width of fabric; subcut into 40 squares 3⅞″ × 3⅞″ and cut each square diagonally once to form 80 small triangles.

From binding fabric:

- Cut 6 strips 2¼″ × width of fabric and continue as instructed in Binding (page 32).

From backing fabric:

- Cut 2 pieces 57″ × width of fabric. Sew together the pieces to form a horizontal seam in the backing.

Petal Construction

Refer to Appliqué Basics (page 8) as needed.

1. Use the petal pattern (page 84) to trace 160 petals onto the fusible web. Use the petal placement guide (page 10) for optimal petal placement.

2. Cut out the petals and trim the interior of each petal (page 10).

3. Fuse the petals onto the wrong side of the scrap fabrics. If you are using precut squares, fuse 2 petals per square.

4. Cut out the fabric petals, remove the paper backing, and set them aside.

Block Construction

Note: All sewing is done right sides together with a ¼″ seam allowance, unless otherwise noted.

1. Sew large triangles to the sides of a 4¾″ × 4¾″ light background square. Press the seams open. Repeat to make a total of 40 units.

Make 40.

2. Sew a small triangle to a unit made in Step 1. Press the seam open. Repeat for each unit.

Add small triangle.

3. Sew light 4³⁄₄″ × 4³⁄₄″ squares to the sides of a 4³⁄₄″ × 4³⁄₄″ medium-light square. Press the seams open. Repeat to make a total of 20 units.

4. Sew 2 units made in Step 2 to the top and bottom of a unit made in Step 3. Press the seams open. Repeat to make a total of 20 units.

5. Sew small triangles to the sides of the unit from Step 3 to complete the block. Repeat to make 20 blocks 12½″ × 12½″. Press the seams open.

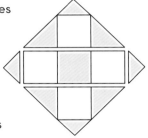

Quilt block assembly

Adding the Appliqué

1. Fuse 8 petals onto each block, following the seamlines. Allow a ¼″ seam allowance around the perimeter of the block.

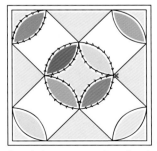

Petal placement and appliqué stitching guide

2. Finish the appliqué edges as desired (pages 12–16). Begin and end the stitching at the X. Stitch the outer petals individually.

Quilt Top Assembly

1. Sew together the blocks in 5 rows of 4 blocks each. Press the seams in adjoining rows in opposite directions.

2. Sew together the rows. Press the seams in one direction.

Finishing It

Refer to Quilt Finishing (pages 28–33) as needed.

1. Layer the backing, the batting, and the quilt top. Baste and quilt as desired.

2. Trim the excess batting and backing from the quilt and bind.

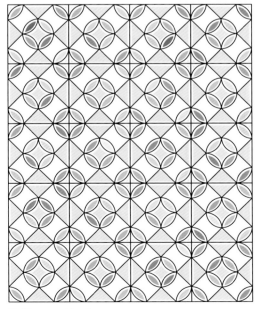

Quilt assembly diagram

Oh, how I love scraps! I always have an overflowing bin of small scraps that I can't bear to throw away. These fabric bits are really too small to save, but too pretty to toss. Enter the scrappy quilt— a quilt made up of all the best bits.

Scattered Blossoms Pillow

Finished pillow: 18" × 18"   *Finished block:* 12" × 12"

Fabrics: A mix of fabrics from my scrap bin

Pieced and quilted by Corey Yoder

Materials

- Scraps for petals
- ¼ yard fabric for background
- ⅓ yard polka dot fabric for pieced block and corner squares
- ¼ yard fabric for binding
- ½ yard fabric for backing
- ⅓ yard fusible web (based on 17″ width)
- 20″ × 20″ piece of batting
- 20″ × 20″ piece of muslin for pillow sandwich
- 18″ × 18″ square pillow form

Cutting Instructions

From background fabric:

- Cut 1 square 7¼″ × 7¼″; cut diagonally twice to form 4 large triangles.
- Cut 2 strips 3½″ × remaining width of fabric; subcut into 4 rectangles 3½″ × 12½″.

From polka dot fabric:

- Cut 1 strip 4¾″ × width of fabric; subcut into 5 squares 4¾″ × 4¾″.

- Cut 1 strip 3⅞″ × width of fabric; subcut into 2 squares 3⅞″ × 3⅞″ and cut each square diagonally once to form 4 small triangles. From the remaining strip, cut 4 squares 3½″ × 3½″.

From binding fabric:

- Cut 2 strips 2¼″ × width of fabric and continue as instructed in Binding (page 32).

From backing fabric:

- Cut 2 rectangles 12½″ × 18½″ and continue as instructed in Pillow Back (page 34).

Petal and Block Construction

1. Refer to Petal Construction (page 79). The pillow pattern uses 20 petals.

2. Refer to Block Construction (page 79) to make 1 block 12½″ × 12½″.

Pillow Top Assembly

1. Sew 3½" × 12½" background rectangles to the sides of the 12½" × 12½" block. Press the seams away from the center.

2. Sew 3½" × 3½" polka dot squares to the ends of the 2 remaining rectangles. Press the seams toward the background fabric.

3. Sew the units made in Step 2 to the top and bottom of the unit made in Step 1. Press the seams away from the center.

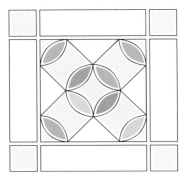

Pillow assembly diagram

Adding the Appliqué

Refer to Adding the Appliqué (page 80) for fusing the petals. In addition, fuse 3 petals in each corner of the pillow top border as illustrated.

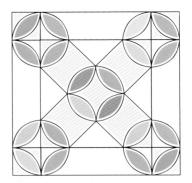

Fuse corner petals.

Finishing It

Refer to Pillow Finishing (page 34) as needed.

1. Layer the pillow top, the batting, and the muslin.

2. Quilt as desired.

3. Layer the quilted pillow top and the 2 backing pieces. Pin into place, baste, and bind.

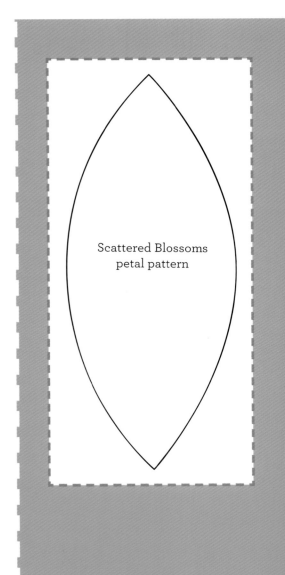

Scattered Blossoms petal pattern

Polka dots and flowers—two of my favorite things! Use any of your favorite fabrics for this cheery pillow.

Petal Path Quilt

Finished quilt: 72½″ × 72½″   *Finished block:* 12″ × 12″

Fabrics: Avignon by Emily Taylor for Riley Blake Designs

Pieced by Corey Yoder • Quilted by Natalia Bonner

Materials

- 4½ yards fabric for background
- 4½ yards solid fabric for diagonal frames
- ¼ yard each of 18 print fabrics or 18 fat quarters for petals and pieced blocks
- ⅔ yard fabric for binding
- 4½ yards fabric for backing
- 4 yards fusible web (based on 17″ width)
- 80″ × 80″ piece of batting

Cutting Instructions

From background fabric:

- Cut 12 strips 12½″ × width of fabric; subcut into 36 squares 12½″ × 12½″.

From frame fabric:

- Cut 18 strips 8½″ × width of fabric; subcut into 72 squares 8½″ × 8½″ and mark a diagonal line on the wrong side of each square.

From each petal fabric:

- Cut 4 squares 5½″ × 5½″, mark a diagonal line on the wrong side of each square, and set aside the remaining fabric to use for petals.

  Note: If you are using fat quarters, use this fat quarter cutting guide.

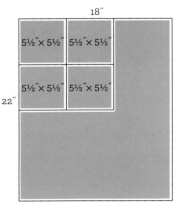

Fat quarter cutting guide

From binding fabric:

- Cut 8 strips 2¼″ × width of fabric and continue as instructed in Binding (page 32).

From backing fabric:

- Cut 2 pieces 81″ × width of fabric. Sew together the pieces to form a horizontal seam in the backing.

Petal Construction

Refer to Appliqué Basics (page 8) as needed.

1. Use the petal pattern (page 90) to trace 72 petals onto the fusible web. Use the petal placement guide (page 10) for optimal petal placement.

2. Cut out the petals and trim the interior of each petal (page 10).

3. Fuse 4 petals to the wrong side of each petal fabric.

4. Cut out the fabric petals, remove the paper backing, and set them aside.

Block Construction

Note: All sewing is done right sides together with a ¼" seam allowance, unless otherwise noted.

1. Place an 8½" × 8½" solid square right sides together with a 12½" × 12½" background square. Refer to the illustration for square placement and orientation.

2. Sew together the pieces on the marked line. Trim the excess fabric, leaving a ¼" seam allowance. Press the seams open.

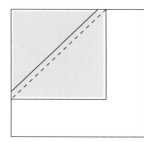

3. Repeat Steps 1 and 2 with another 8½" × 8½" solid square in the opposite corner.

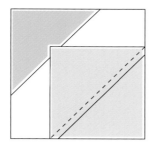

4. Repeat Steps 1–3 to make 36 units.

5. Place 5½" × 5½" print squares on the unit from the previous steps. Refer to the illustration for square placement and orientation.

6. Sew on the marked line. Trim the excess fabric, leaving a ¼" seam allowance. Press the seams open.

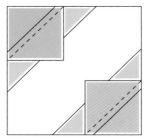

Make 36.

7. Repeat Steps 5 and 6 to make 36 blocks 12½" × 12½".

Adding the Appliqué

1. Center and fuse 2 petals onto each block. Allow a ¼" seam allowance around the perimeter of the block.

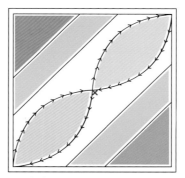

Petal placement and appliqué stitching guide

2. Finish the appliqué edges as desired (pages 12–16). Begin and end the stitching at the X.

Super-sized petals are a great way to show off both large- and small-scale prints. Usually I look for small-print fabrics to work with smaller appliqué pieces, but I love that the large petals in this quilt allow bigger-print fabrics to sing. The solids incorporated into the quilt perfectly frame all the lively prints.

Petal Path
petal pattern

Quilt Top Assembly

1. Sew together the blocks in 6 rows of 6 blocks each. Press the seams in adjoining rows in opposite directions.

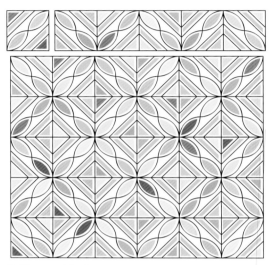

Quilt assembly diagram

2. Sew together the rows. Press the seams in one direction.

Finishing It

Refer to Quilt Finishing (pages 28–33) as needed.

1. Layer the backing, the batting, and the quilt top. Baste and quilt as desired.

2. Trim the excess batting and backing from the quilt and bind.

Petal Path Pillow

Finished pillow: 24″ × 24″   *Finished block:* 12″ × 12″

Fabrics: California Girl and Avalon, both by Fig Tree Quilts for Moda Fabrics;
Annie's Farm Stand by Holly Holderman for Lakehouse Fabrics;
and Echo by Lotta Jansdotter for Windham Fabrics

Pieced and quilted by Corey Yoder

Materials

- ⅓ yard print fabric for petals
- ¾ yard solid fabric for background
- ⅓ yard fabric for inner frame
- ⅓ yard fabric for outer frame
- ¼ yard fabric for binding
- ¾ yard fabric for backing
- ½ yard fusible web (based on 17″ width)
- 26″ × 26″ piece of batting
- 26″ × 26″ piece of muslin for pillow sandwich
- 24″ × 24″ square pillow form

Cutting Instructions

From background fabric:

- Cut 2 strips 12½" × width of fabric; subcut the first strip into 3 squares 12½" × 12½" and subcut the second strip into 1 square 12½" × 12½" and 8 squares 5½" × 5½".

From each of 2 frame fabrics:

- Cut 1 strip 8½" × width of fabric; subcut into 4 squares 8½" × 8½".

From binding fabric:

- Cut 3 strips 2¼" × width of fabric and continue as instructed in Binding (page 32).

From backing fabric:

- Cut 2 rectangles 15½" × 24½" and continue as instructed in Pillow Back (page 34).

Petal and Block Construction

1. Refer to Petal Construction (page 87). Use 8 petals.

2. Refer to Block Construction (page 88) to make a total of 4 blocks 12½" × 12½". In Steps 1–4, use a square of each of the frame fabrics; in Steps 5–7, use the solid 5½" × 5½" squares.

Adding the Appliqué

Refer to Adding the Appliqué (page 88) for fusing the petals.

Pillow Top Assembly

1. Sew together the blocks in 2 rows of 2 blocks each. Press the seams in adjoining rows in opposite directions.

2. Sew together the rows. Press the seams in one direction.

Finishing It

Refer to Pillow Finishing (page 34) as needed.

1. Layer the pillow top, the batting, and the muslin.

2. Quilt as desired.

3. Layer the quilted pillow top and the 2 backing pieces. Pin into place, baste, and bind.

In my opinion, you can never own enough text fabrics. I often use them in my quilts and pillows. They are always a welcome addition to any project, whether it's a sharp black-and-white text print or a soft yellow text print like the one used in this pillow.

Sunshine and Clouds Quilt

Finished quilt: 48½" × 60½"   *Finished block:* 12" × 12"

Fabrics: Madrona Road by Violet Craft for Michael Miller Fabrics and
Lark by Amy Butler for Westminster Fabrics

Pieced by Corey Yoder   •   Quilted by Angela Walters

Materials

- 7/8 yard each of 4 different prints or 40 precut 2½"-wide strips (jelly roll) for petals

- 1 yard each of 2 different prints for block centers

- 1¾ yards solid fabric for background

- ½ yard fabric for binding

- 3¼ yards fabric for backing

- 4½ yards fusible web (based on 17" width)

- 56" × 68" piece of batting

Cutting Instructions

From each of 4 petal fabrics:

- Cut 10 strips 2½" × width of fabric (skip if you are using precut strips).

From each block center fabric:

- Cut 3 strips 9" × width of fabric; subcut into 10 squares 9" × 9".

From background fabric:

- Cut 8 strips 6⅞" × width of fabric; subcut into 40 squares 6⅞" × 6⅞" and cut each square diagonally once to make 80 triangles.

From binding fabric:

- Cut 6 strips 2¼" × width of fabric and continue as instructed in Binding (page 32).

From backing fabric:

- Cut 2 pieces 57" × width of fabric. Sew together the pieces to form a horizontal seam in the backing.

Petal Construction

Refer to Appliqué Basics (page 8) as needed.

Note: All sewing is done right sides together with a ¼" seam allowance, unless otherwise noted.

1. Use the petal pattern (page 100) to trace 80 petals onto the fusible web. Use the petal placement guide (page 10) for optimal petal placement.

2. Cut out the petals and trim the interior of each petal (page 10).

3. Pair the 2½" strips and sew them together lengthwise. Press the seams open. Make a total of 20 strip sets.

4. Trim any stray threads along the strip-set seams.

5. Iron the fusible web for 4 petals to the wrong side of each strip set. Align the petal points with the seam.

Align fusible web for petals with seam, 4 petals per strip.

6. Cut out the fabric petals, remove the paper backing, and set them aside.

Block Construction

Note: All sewing is done right sides together with a ¼″ seam allowance, unless otherwise noted.

1. Sew background triangles to the sides of each 9″ × 9″ center block square. Press the seams open.

2. Sew background triangles to the top and bottom of a unit made in Step 1. Press the seams open. Repeat to make 20 blocks 12½″ × 12½″.

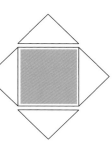

Make 20.

Adding the Appliqué

1. Fuse 4 petals to each block, aligning the petal seam with the block seam. Allow a ¼″ seam allowance around the perimeter of the block.

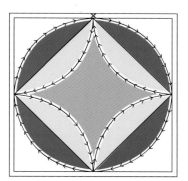

Petal placement and appliqué stitching guide

2. Finish the appliqué edges as desired (pages 12–16). Begin and end the stitching at the X.

Quilt Top Assembly

1. Sew together the blocks in 5 rows of 4 blocks each. Press the seams in adjoining rows in opposite directions.

2. Sew together the rows. Press the seams in one direction.

Finishing It

Refer to Quilt Finishing (pages 28–33) as needed.

1. Layer the backing, the batting, and the quilt top. Baste and quilt as desired.

2. Trim the excess batting and backing from the quilt and bind.

Quilt assembly diagram

Scale plays a very important role when choosing fabrics for any quilt. Sunshine and Clouds provides a perfect opportunity to display a favorite large-scale fabric (or two) in the block centers. The split petals are so easy to make, yet they totally transform the look of the petals. Use jelly roll strips for a scrappy quilt or choose six coordinating fabrics and you'll be on your way to a dynamite quilt!

Sunshine and Clouds Pillow

Finished pillow: 18″ × 18″   *Finished block:* 12″ × 12″

Fabrics: Lucy's Crab Shack by Sweetwater for Moda Fabrics

Pieced and quilted by Corey Yoder

Materials

- ⅛ yard each of 2 different solids for petals

- ⅓ yard fabric for block center (½ yard if fussy cutting directional print as shown)

- ¼ yard solid fabric for background and first border

- ¼ yard fabric for second border

- ¼ yard fabric for binding

- ½ yard fabric for backing

- ¼ yard fusible web (based on 17" width)

- 20" × 20" piece of batting

- 20" × 20" piece of muslin for pillow sandwich

- 18" × 18" square pillow form

tip For this project I really wanted to use a white fabric on top of the navy text print. However, the text print was quite visible through the white fabric, which I didn't care for. To work around this, I fused two pieces of white fabric together prior to making my strip set.

Cutting Instructions

From each of 2 petal fabrics:

- Cut 1 strip 2½" × width of fabric.

From block center fabric:

- Cut 1 square 9" × 9".

From background / first border fabric:

- Cut 1 strip 6⅞" × width of fabric; subcut into 2 squares 6⅞" × 6⅞" and cut each square diagonally once.

- Cut 2 strips 1½" × remaining width of fabric; subcut into 2 rectangles 1½" × 12½" and 2 rectangles 1½" × 14½".

From second border fabric:

- Cut 2 strips 2½" × width of fabric; subcut into 2 rectangles 2½" × 14½" and 2 rectangles 2½" × 18½".

From binding fabric:

- Cut 2 strips 2¼" × width of fabric and continue as instructed in Binding (page 32).

From backing fabric:

- Cut 2 rectangles 12½" × 18½" and continue as instructed in Pillow Back (page 34).

Petal and Block Construction

1. Refer to Petal Construction (page 95). The pillow pattern uses 4 petals in Step 1 and 1 strip set in Step 3.

2. Refer to Block Construction (page 96) to make 1 block 12½" × 12½".

Sunshine and Clouds
petal pattern

Pillow Top Assembly

1. Sew 1½″ × 12½″ border pieces to the sides of the 12½″ × 12½″ pillow center. Press the seams away from the center. Sew 1½″ × 14½″ border pieces to the top and bottom of the pillow center. Press the seams away from the center.

2. Sew 2½″ × 14½″ second border pieces to the sides of the unit made in Step 1. Press the seams away from the center. Sew 2½″ × 18½″ border pieces to the top and bottom of the pillow. Press the seams away from the center.

Pillow assembly diagram

Adding the Appliqué

Refer to Adding the Appliqué (page 96) for fusing the petals.

Finishing It

Refer to Pillow Finishing (page 34) as needed.

1. Layer the pillow top, the batting, and the muslin.

2. Quilt as desired.

3. Layer the quilted pillow top and the 2 backing pieces. Pin into place, baste, and bind.

Split petals take center stage in this pillow. Choose your favorite fabric for the center, add some big stitches, and you'll get WOW!

Posey Patch Quilt

Finished quilt: 48½" × 60½"   *Finished block:* 12" × 12"

Fabrics: Pure Elements Solids by Art Gallery Fabrics and
Cotton Couture Solids by Michael Miller Fabrics

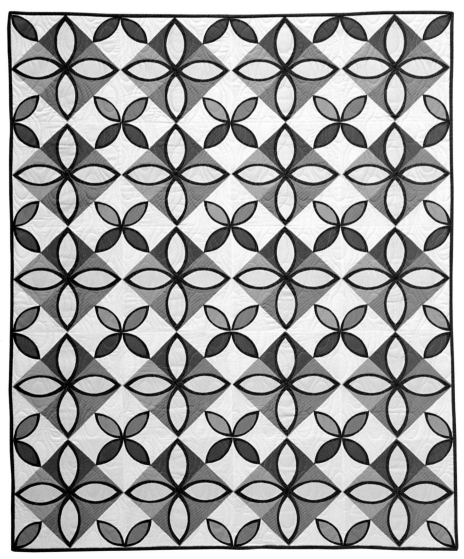

Pieced by Corey Yoder • Quilted by Natalia Bonner

Materials

- ½ yard each of 4 different solid fabrics (yellow, dark pink, light pink, orange) for pieced squares

- 2½ yards white solid fabric for background and petals

- 1½ yards gray solid fabric for petals

- ¼ yard each of 4 different solid fabrics (purple, light green, aqua, emerald) for petals

- ½ yard fabric for binding

- 3¼ yards fabric for backing

- 5 yards fusible web (based on 17″ width)

- 56″ × 68″ piece of batting

Cutting Instructions

From each of 4 pieced square solid fabrics:

- Cut 3 strips 4¾″ × width of fabric; subcut into 20 squares 4¾″ × 4¾″.

From background fabric:

- Cut 8 strips 6⅞″ × width of fabric; subcut into 40 squares 6⅞″ × 6⅞″ and cut each square diagonally once to form 80 triangles. Set aside the remaining fabric for the petals.

From binding fabric:

- Cut 6 strips 2¼″ × width of fabric and continue as instructed in Binding (page 32).

From backing fabric:

- Cut 2 pieces 57″ × width of fabric. Sew together the pieces to form a horizontal seam in the backing.

Petal Construction

Refer to Appliqué Basics (page 8) as needed.

1. Use the 4 petal patterns (pages 106 and 110) to trace 80 petals of each of the 4 sizes onto the fusible web. Use the petal placement guide (page 10) for optimal petal placement.

2. Cut out the petals and trim the interior of each petal (page 10).

3. Fuse 20 small petals onto each ¼ yard of solid fabric. Fuse 80 medium petals and 80 extra-large petals onto the gray solid fabric. Fuse 80 large petals onto the white solid fabric.

4. Cut out the fabric petals, remove the paper backing, and set them aside.

Block Construction

Note: All sewing is done right sides together with a ¼″ seam allowance, unless otherwise noted.

1. Sew together a yellow 4¾″ × 4¾″ square and a dark pink 4¾″ × 4¾″ square. Press the seam toward the yellow square. Repeat to make 20 units.

2. Sew together a light pink 4¾″ × 4¾″ square and an orange 4¾″ × 4¾″ square. Press the seam toward the orange square. Repeat to make 20 units.

3. Sew together a unit made in Step 1 and a unit made in Step 2. Press the seam in one direction. Repeat to make 20 units.

Make 20 four-patch units.

4. Center and sew white triangles to the top and bottom of each four-patch. Press the seams open.

5. Center and sew white triangles to the sides of a unit made in Step 4. Press the seams open. Repeat to make 20 blocks 12½″ × 12½″.

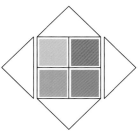

Make 20.

Adding the Appliqué

1. Fuse 4 extra-large gray petals onto the four-patch squares. Fuse 4 medium gray petals onto each corner. Allow a ¼″ seam allowance around the perimeter of the block.

Petal placement and appliqué stitching guide

2. Fuse 4 large white petals onto the center of the extra-large gray petals. Stitch each of these petals individually.

3. Fuse a small petal onto the center of each medium gray petal. Stitch each of these petals individually.

Make 20.

4. Finish the appliqué edges as desired (pages 12–16). Begin and end the stitching at the X.

Stacked petals create so many more design options! As I was designing the projects for this book, I couldn't wait to make this quilt. It requires a lot of appliqué, but the end results are so worth it. I love all the projects in this book, but I saved my favorite for last.

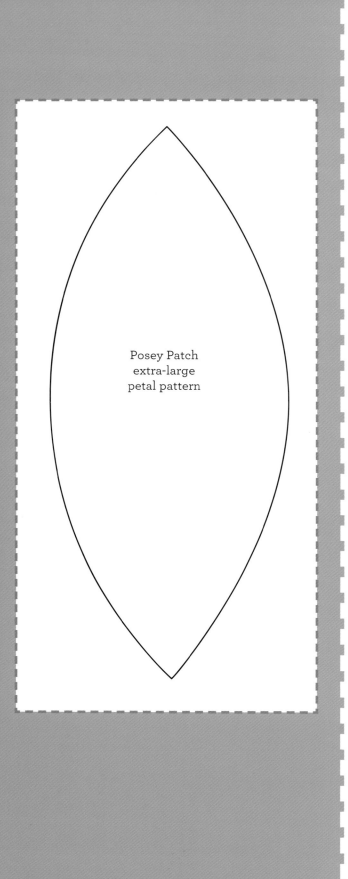

Posey Patch
extra-large
petal pattern

Quilt Top Assembly

1. Sew together the blocks in 5 rows of 4 blocks each. Press the seams in adjoining rows in opposite directions.

2. Sew together the rows. Press the seams in one direction.

Finishing It

Refer to Quilt Finishing (pages 28–33) as needed.

1. Layer the backing, the batting, and the quilt top. Baste and quilt as desired.

2. Trim the excess batting and backing from the quilt and bind.

Quilt assembly diagram

Posey Patch Pillow

Finished pillow: 18″ × 18″ *Finished block:* 12″ × 12″

Fabrics: From various collections by Denyse Schmidt

Pieced and quilted by Corey Yoder

Materials

- Fabric scraps for small and large petals
- ¼ yard white solid fabric for medium petals
- 4 squares 4¾″ × 4¾″ of print fabric for pieced center
- ½ yard solid fabric for background and extra-large petals
- ¼ yard fabric for binding
- ½ yard fabric for backing
- ⅔ yard fusible web (based on 17″ width)
- 20″ × 20″ piece of batting
- 20″ × 20″ piece of muslin for pillow sandwich
- 18″ × 18″ square pillow form

Cutting Instructions

From background fabric:

- Cut 1 strip 6⅞″ × width of fabric; subcut into 2 squares 6⅞″ × 6⅞″ and cut each square diagonally once to form 4 triangles. Set aside the remaining fabric for the petal construction.
- Cut 2 strips 3½″ × width of fabric; subcut into 2 rectangles 3½″ × 12½″ and 2 rectangles 3½″ × 18½″.

From binding fabric:

- Cut 2 strips 2¼″ × width of fabric and continue as instructed in Binding (page 32).

From backing fabric:

- Cut 2 rectangles 12½″ × 18½″ and continue as instructed in Pillow Back (page 34).

Petal and Block Construction

1. Refer to Petal Construction (page 103). Use 4 each of the large and extra-large petals and 16 each of the small and medium petals.

Use the ¼ yard of white solid petal fabric for the medium petals, the fabric scraps for the large and small petals, and the background fabric for the extra-large petals.

2. Refer to Block Construction (page 104) to make 1 block 12½″ × 12½″.

Pillow Top Assembly

Note: All sewing is done right sides together with a ¼″ seam allowance, unless otherwise noted.

1. Sew 3½″ × 12½″ background rectangles to the sides of the 12½″ × 12½″ block. Press the seams away from the center.

2. Sew 3½″ × 18½″ background rectangles to the top and bottom of the unit made in Step 1. Press the seams away from the center.

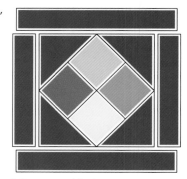

Pillow assembly diagram

Change things up a bit by using prints instead of solids. Choose the fabrics carefully, as bold prints or colors will show through when layered under lighter colors.

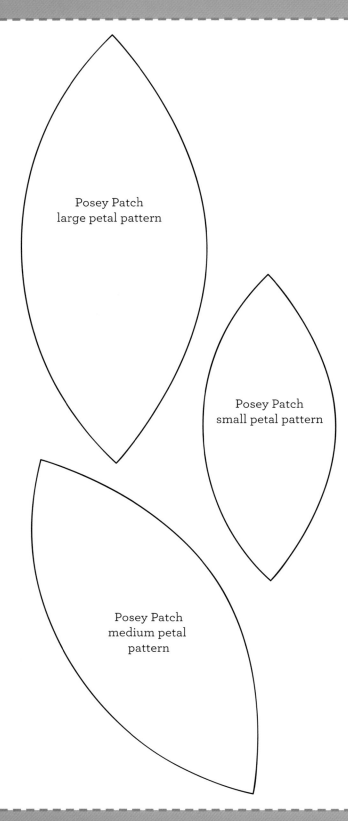

Posey Patch
large petal pattern

Posey Patch
small petal pattern

Posey Patch
medium petal
pattern

Adding the Appliqué

1. Refer to Adding the Appliqué (page 104) for fusing the petals. In addition, fuse 3 medium petals and 3 small petals in each corner of the pillow top border as illustrated. Allow a ¼" seam allowance around the perimeter of the pillow top.

Border petal placement

2. Finish the appliqué edges as desired (pages 12–16).

Finishing It

Refer to Pillow Finishing (page 34) as needed.

1. Layer the pillow top, the batting, and the muslin.

2. Quilt as desired.

3. Layer the quilted pillow top and the 2 backing pieces. Pin into place, baste, and bind.